Collins
INTERNATIONAL PRIMARY SCIENCE

Teacher's Guide 4

William Collins' dream of knowledge for all began with the publication of his first book in 1819. A self-educated mill worker, he not only enriched millions of lives, but also founded a flourishing publishing house. Today, staying true to this spirit, Collins books are packed with inspiration, innovation and practical expertise. They place you at the centre of a world of possibility and give you exactly what you need to explore it.

Collins. Freedom to teach.

Published by Collins
An imprint of HarperCollins*Publishers* Ltd.
The News Building
1 London Bridge Street
London
SE1 9GF

Browse the complete Collins catalogue at
www.collins.co.uk

© HarperCollins*Publishers* Limited 2014

10 9 8 7 6 5

ISBN: 978-0-00-758621-9

The authors assert their moral rights to be identified as the authors of this work.

Contributing authors: Karen Morrison, Tracey Baxter, Sunetra Berry, Pat Dower, Helen Harden, Pauline Hannigan, Anita Loughrey, Emily Miller, Jonathan Miller, Anne Pilling, Pete Robinson.

The exam-style questions and sample answers used in the Assessment Sheets have been written by the author.

Any educational institution that has purchased one copy of this publication may make unlimited duplicate copies for use exclusively within that institution. Permission does not extend to reproduction, storage within a retrieval system, or transmittal in any form or by any means, electronic, mechanical, photocopying, recording or otherwise, of duplicate copies for loaning, renting or selling to any other institution without the permission of the Publisher.

British Library Cataloguing in Publication Data
A Catalogue record for this publication is available from the British Library.

Commissioned by Elizabeth Catford
Project managed by Karen Williams
Design and production by Ken Vail Graphic Design

Acknowledgements
The publishers wish to thank the following for permission to reproduce photographs.
Every effort has been made to trace copyright holders and to obtain their permission for the use of copyright materials. The publishers will gladly receive any information enabling them to rectify any error or omission at the first opportunity.

COVER: photo: iurii / Shutterstock.com

All other photos Shutterstock.

FSC is a non-profit international organisation established to promote the responsible management of the world's forests. Products carrying the FSC label are independently certified to assure consumers that they come from forests that are managed to meet the social, economic and ecological needs of present and future generations, and other controlled sources.

Contents

Introduction	v
Teacher's Guide	vi
Student's Book	viii
Workbook	x
DVD	xi
Assessment in primary science	xii
Learning objectives matching grid	xiv
Scientific enquiry skills matching grid	xvi

Lesson plans

Topic 1 Humans and animals

1.1	Animal skeletons	2
1.2	Your skeleton	4
1.3	Growing bones	6
1.4	Functions of the skeleton	8
1.5	Protecting your organs	10
1.6	Muscles	12
1.7	Moving your bones	14
1.8	Investigating moving bones	16
1.9	Drugs and medicines	18
1.10	Different medicines	20
	Consolidation and Assessment Sheet answers	22
	Student's Book answers	23

Topic 2 Living things in their environment

2.1	The importance of the environment	24
2.2	Adapting to different habitats	26
2.3	Investigating different habitats	28
2.4	Identifying and grouping animals	30
2.5	Using identification keys	32
2.6	Human activity and the environment	34
2.7	Waste and recycling	36
	Consolidation and Assessment Sheet answers	38
	Student's Book answers	39

iii

Topic 3 States of matter

3.1	States of matter	40
3.2	Water	42
3.3	Heating matter	44
3.4	Cooling matter	46
3.5	Liquid to gas	48
3.6	Gas to liquid	50
	Consolidation and Assessment Sheet answers	52
	Student's Book answers	53

Topic 4 Sound

4.1	How sounds are made	54
4.2	Measuring sound	56
4.3	Sound travels through different materials	58
4.4	Reducing sound levels	60
4.5	Soundproofing materials	62
4.6	Musical instruments	64
4.7	Pitch	66
4.8	Changing the pitch of a musical instrument	68
	Consolidation and Assessment Sheet answers	70
	Student's Book answers	71

Topic 5 Electricity and magnetism

5.1	Electrical circuits	72
5.2	Building circuits	74
5.3	Why won't it work?	76
5.4	Electrical current	78
5.5	Magnets	80
5.6	Investigate magnetic forces	82
5.7	Magnets and metals	84
5.8	Using magnets to sort metals	86
	Consolidation and Assessment Sheet answers	88
	Student's Book answers	89

Photocopy Masters   90
Assessment Sheets   102

Introduction

About *Collins International Primary Science*

Collins International Primary Science is specifically written to fully meet the requirements of the Cambridge Primary Science curriculum framework from Cambridge International Examinations and the material has been carefully developed to meet the needs of primary science students and teachers in a range of international contexts.

Content is organised according to the three main strands: Biology, Chemistry and Physics and the skills detailed under the Scientific Enquiry strand are introduced and taught in the context of those areas.

All course materials make use of the fully-integrated digital resources available on the DVD. For example, video clips and slideshows allow students the opportunity to view at first-hand examples of habitats, plants and animals they may not be familiar with from their own country. The interactive activities provide a valuable teaching resource that will engage the students and consolidate learning.

Components of the course

For each of Stages 1 to 6 as detailed in the Cambridge Primary Science Framework, we offer:

- A full colour, highly illustrated and photograph rich Student's Book
- A write-in Workbook linked to the Student's Book
- This comprehensive Teacher's Guide with clear suggestions for using the materials, including the electronic components of the course
- A DVD which contains slideshows, video clips, additional photographs and interactive activities for use in the classroom.

Approach

The course is designed with student-centred learning at its heart. The students conduct investigations with guidance and support from their teacher. Their investigations respond to questions asked by the teacher or asked by the students themselves. They are practical and activity-based, and include observing, questioning, making and testing predictions, collecting and recording simple data, observing patterns and suggesting explanations. Plenty of opportunity is provided for the students to consolidate and apply what they have learned and to relate what they are doing in science to other curriculum areas and the environment in which they live.

Much of the students' work is conducted as paired work or in small groups, in line with international best practice. Activities are designed to be engaging for students and to support teachers in their assessment of student progress and achievement. Each lesson is planned to support clear learning objectives and outcomes, to provide students and teachers with a good view of the learning. The activities within each unit provide opportunities for oral and written feedback by the teacher, peer teaching and peer assessment within small groups.

Throughout the course there is wide variety of learning experiences on offer. The materials are structured so that they do not impose a rigid structure but rather provide a range of options linked to the learning objectives. Teachers are able to select from these to provide an interesting, exciting and appropriate learning experience that is suited to their particular classroom situations.

Differentiation

Differentiation is clearly built into the lesson plans in this Teacher's Guide and levels are indicated against the Student's Book activities. You will see that the practical activities offer three levels of differentiated demand. The square activities are appropriate for the level of nearly all of the students. The circle questions are appropriate for the level of most of the students (this is the level students should be achieving for this stage). The triangle questions are appropriate for some students of higher ability. Teachers may find that achievement levels vary for different content strands and interest levels. So students who are working at the circle level in Biology may find Chemistry or Physics topics more interesting and/or easier, so they may work at a different level for some of the time.

Teacher's Guide

Each double-page spread covers one unit in the Student's Book. Each unit has a clear structure identified by the *Introduction–Teaching and learning activities–Consolidate and review* sequence.

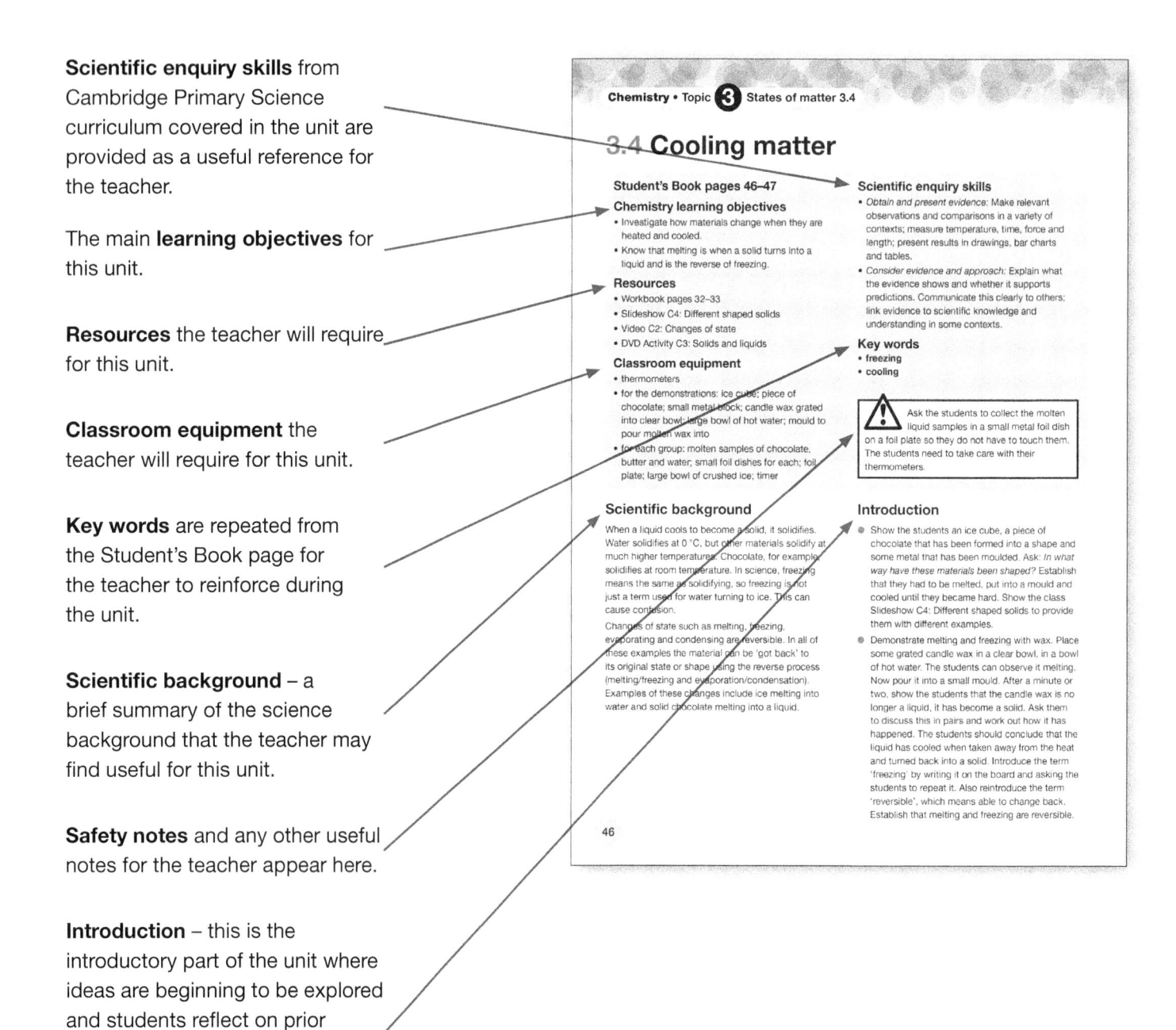

Scientific enquiry skills from Cambridge Primary Science curriculum covered in the unit are provided as a useful reference for the teacher.

The main **learning objectives** for this unit.

Resources the teacher will require for this unit.

Classroom equipment the teacher will require for this unit.

Key words are repeated from the Student's Book page for the teacher to reinforce during the unit.

Scientific background – a brief summary of the science background that the teacher may find useful for this unit.

Safety notes and any other useful notes for the teacher appear here.

Introduction – this is the introductory part of the unit where ideas are beginning to be explored and students reflect on prior learning and share objectives.

Chemistry • Topic 3 States of matter 3.4

3.4 Cooling matter

Student's Book pages 46–47

Chemistry learning objectives
- Investigate how materials change when they are heated and cooled.
- Know that melting is when a solid turns into a liquid and is the reverse of freezing.

Resources
- Workbook pages 32–33
- Slideshow C4: Different shaped solids
- Video C2: Changes of state
- DVD Activity C3: Solids and liquids

Classroom equipment
- thermometers
- for the demonstrations: ice cube; piece of chocolate; small metal block; candle wax grated into clear bowl; large bowl of hot water; mould to pour molten wax into
- for each group: molten samples of chocolate, butter and water; small foil dishes for each; foil plate; large bowl of crushed ice; timer

Scientific background

When a liquid cools to become a solid, it solidifies. Water solidifies at 0 °C, but other materials solidify at much higher temperatures. Chocolate, for example, solidifies at room temperature. In science, freezing means the same as solidifying, so freezing is not just a term used for water turning to ice. This can cause confusion.

Changes of state such as melting, freezing, evaporating and condensing are reversible. In all of these examples the material can be 'got back' to its original state or shape using the reverse process (melting/freezing and evaporation/condensation). Examples of these changes include ice melting into water and solid chocolate melting into a liquid.

Scientific enquiry skills
- *Obtain and present evidence:* Make relevant observations and comparisons in a variety of contexts; measure temperature, time, force and length; present results in drawings, bar charts and tables.
- *Consider evidence and approach:* Explain what the evidence shows and whether it supports predictions. Communicate this clearly to others; link evidence to scientific knowledge and understanding in some contexts.

Key words
- freezing
- cooling

⚠ Ask the students to collect the molten liquid samples in a small metal foil dish on a foil plate so they do not have to touch them. The students need to take care with their thermometers.

Introduction
- Show the students an ice cube, a piece of chocolate that has been formed into a shape and some metal that has been moulded. Ask: *In what way have these materials been shaped?* Establish that they had to be melted, put into a mould and cooled until they became hard. Show the class Slideshow C4: Different shaped solids to provide them with different examples.
- Demonstrate melting and freezing with wax. Place some grated candle wax in a clear bowl, in a bowl of hot water. The students can observe it melting. Now pour it into a small mould. After a minute or two, show the students that the candle wax is no longer a liquid, it has become a solid. Ask them to discuss this in pairs and work out how it has happened. The students should conclude that the liquid has cooled when taken away from the heat and turned back into a solid. Introduce the term 'freezing' by writing it on the board and asking the students to repeat it. Also reintroduce the term 'reversible', which means able to change back. Establish that melting and freezing are reversible.

46

Teacher's Guide

Teaching and learning activities
– this leads into the main lesson.

The **Consolidate and review** section is used to reinforce the students' learning during the lesson.

Graded activities – these are differentiated to suit three different levels of ability. They will often involve an investigation and practical element.

Differentiation – this section discusses the differentiated learning outcomes and provides the teacher with an idea of the likely behaviours of students of different ability, referencing the square, circle and triangle icons which are used across the course.

Links to the **Collins Big Cat** reading scheme are provided to relate science activities to the English that the students are learning.

At the end of each Topic the answers to the Student's Book questions and Assessment Sheets are given in full.

At the back of this Teacher's Guide are the Photocopy Masters (PCMs) and Assessment Sheets. These can be photocopied and handed out to the students as necessary.

vii

The Student's Book

Each double page spread covers one unit. Each page has photographs or graphics to provide a stimulus for discussions and questions.

Key words – these are the words that the students will learn and use for this unit.

Questions – These can be used as whole class discussion points and also to enable the teacher to assess how well individual students understand the unit.

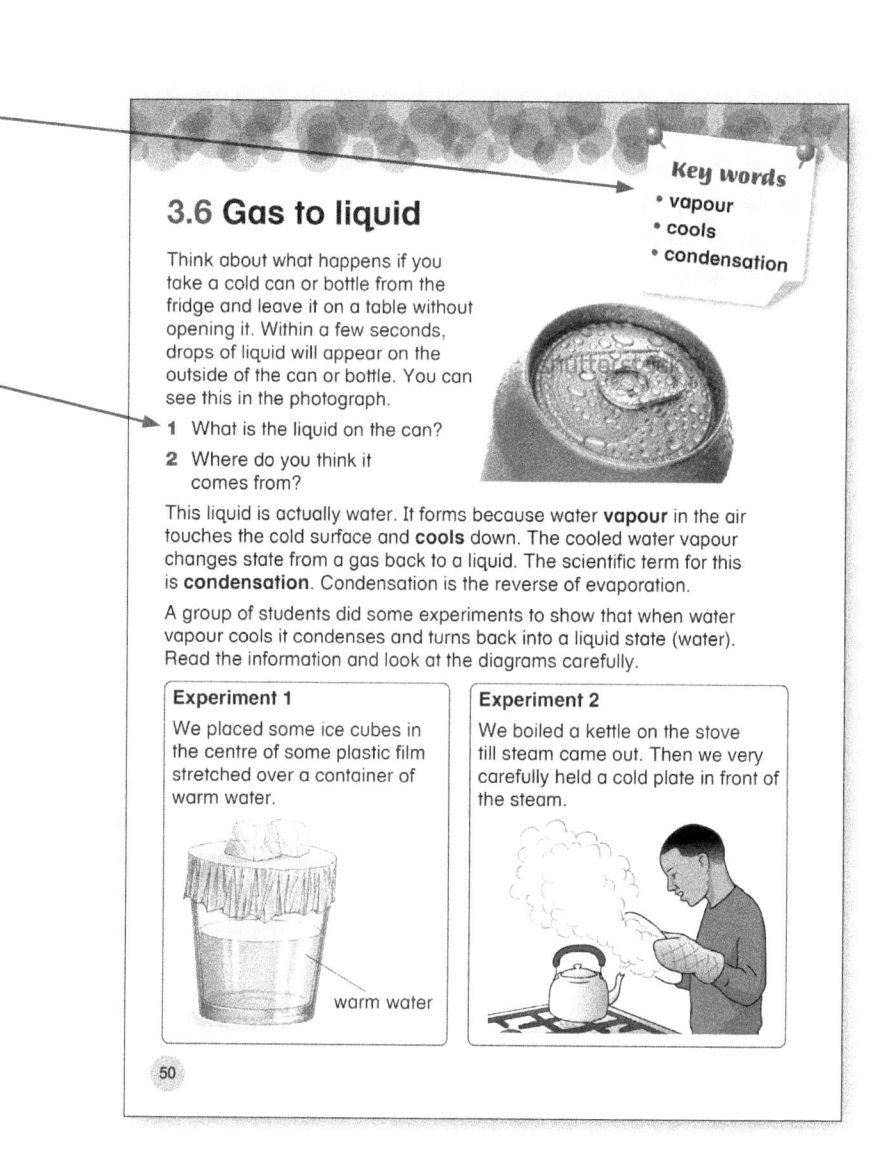

Key words
- vapour
- cools
- condensation

3.6 Gas to liquid

Think about what happens if you take a cold can or bottle from the fridge and leave it on a table without opening it. Within a few seconds, drops of liquid will appear on the outside of the can or bottle. You can see this in the photograph.

1. What is the liquid on the can?
2. Where do you think it comes from?

This liquid is actually water. It forms because water **vapour** in the air touches the cold surface and **cools** down. The cooled water vapour changes state from a gas back to a liquid. The scientific term for this is **condensation**. Condensation is the reverse of evaporation.

A group of students did some experiments to show that when water vapour cools it condenses and turns back into a liquid state (water). Read the information and look at the diagrams carefully.

Experiment 1
We placed some ice cubes in the centre of some plastic film stretched over a container of warm water.

warm water

Experiment 2
We boiled a kettle on the stove till steam came out. Then we very carefully held a cold plate in front of the steam.

50

Student's Book

> **Topic 3 States of matter**
>
> 3 What do you think will happen in each of these experiments?
> 4 Describe how the experiments are different from each other.
> 5 Water droplets form in all three experiments. Where do you think they form? Where do they come from?
>
> **Experiment 3**
> First we rubbed the outside of a can with a duster until it was shiny. Next, we filled the can with ice cubes and then wiped the outside of the can to ensure it was dry. Then we put the can in a warm place. After a few minutes we observed the outside of the can.
>
> **Activities**
>
> 1 Watch the demonstration of each experiment. Record your observations on Workbook page 35.
>
> 2 If water condenses on car windows, the driver cannot see. Find out what drivers can do to prevent the windows from 'misting up'.
>
> 3 Prepare a short presentation to show how evaporation and condensation occur in the water cycle.
>
> **I have learned**
> - Water vapour and steam will turn back into water when they are cooled.
> - This process is called condensation.
>
> 51

Activities

1 Square questions are appropriate for the level of nearly all of the students.

2 Circle questions are appropriate for the level of most of the students (this is the level students should be achieving for this stage).

3 Triangle questions are appropriate for some students of higher ability.

The differentiated activities are usually practical investigations which can be carried out in groups, pairs or as individuals. Guidance and technical advice for these activities is given in the Teacher's Guide.

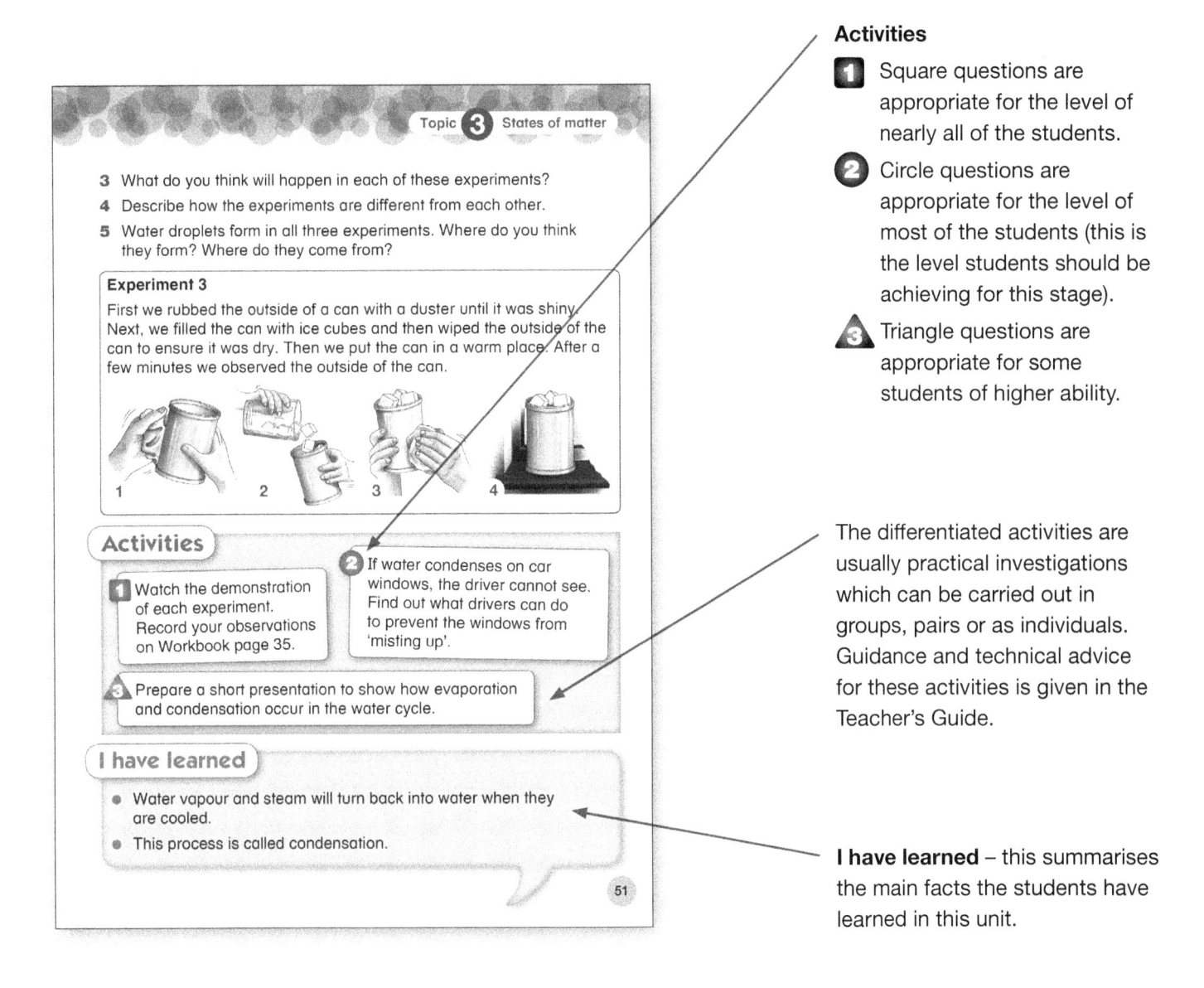

I have learned – this summarises the main facts the students have learned in this unit.

At the back of the Student's Book is a comprehensive **Glossary** of all the Key words that are used during the lessons.

ix

Workbook

The Workbook is for students to record observations, investigation results and key learning during the lesson. It has structured spaces for the students to record work and guidance on what to do. It gives the teacher an opportunity to give the student written feedback and becomes part of each student's work portfolio.

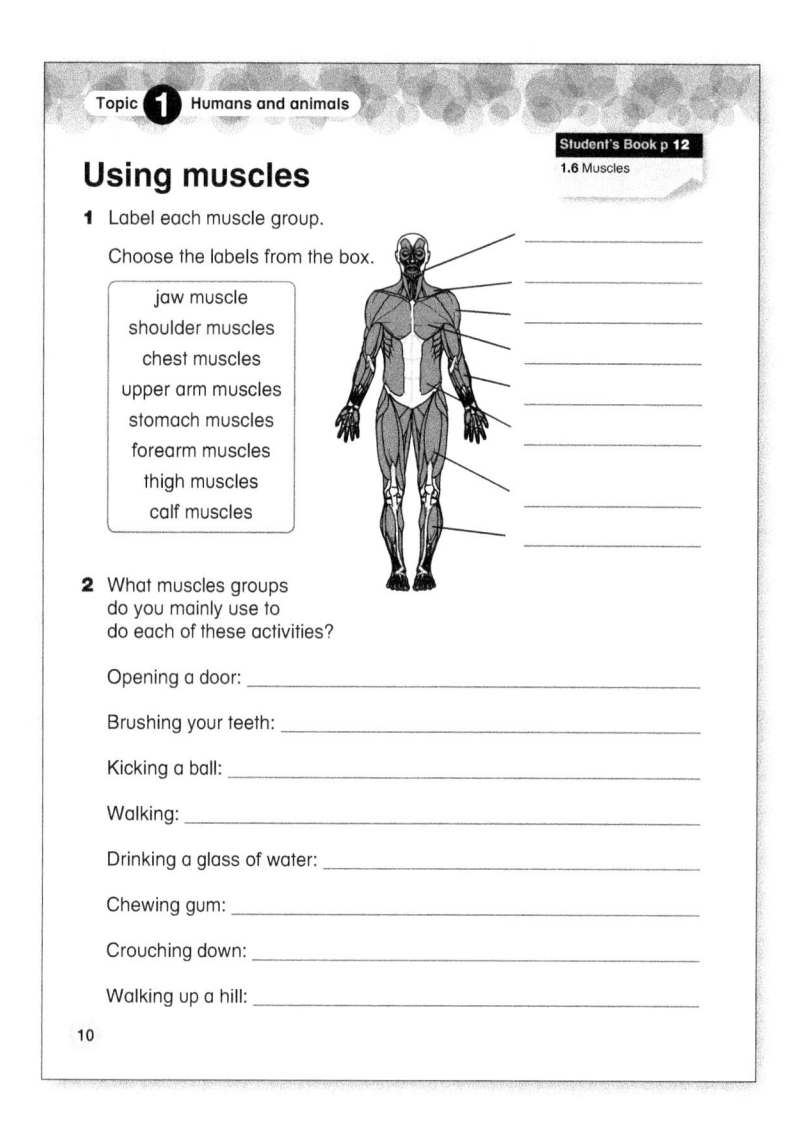

Topic **1** Humans and animals

Student's Book p **12**
1.6 Muscles

Using muscles

1 Label each muscle group.

Choose the labels from the box.

> jaw muscle
> shoulder muscles
> chest muscles
> upper arm muscles
> stomach muscles
> forearm muscles
> thigh muscles
> calf muscles

2 What muscles groups do you mainly use to do each of these activities?

Opening a door: _____

Brushing your teeth: _____

Kicking a ball: _____

Walking: _____

Drinking a glass of water: _____

Chewing gum: _____

Crouching down: _____

Walking up a hill: _____

10

DVD

The DVD provides teachers with a set of electronic resources to support learning and assessment. The lesson plans in this Teacher's Guide give references in the *Resources* box and in the body of text to the relevant video clips, slideshows and interactive 'drag and drop' activities.

Interactive 'drag and drop' activities

Slideshows and video clips

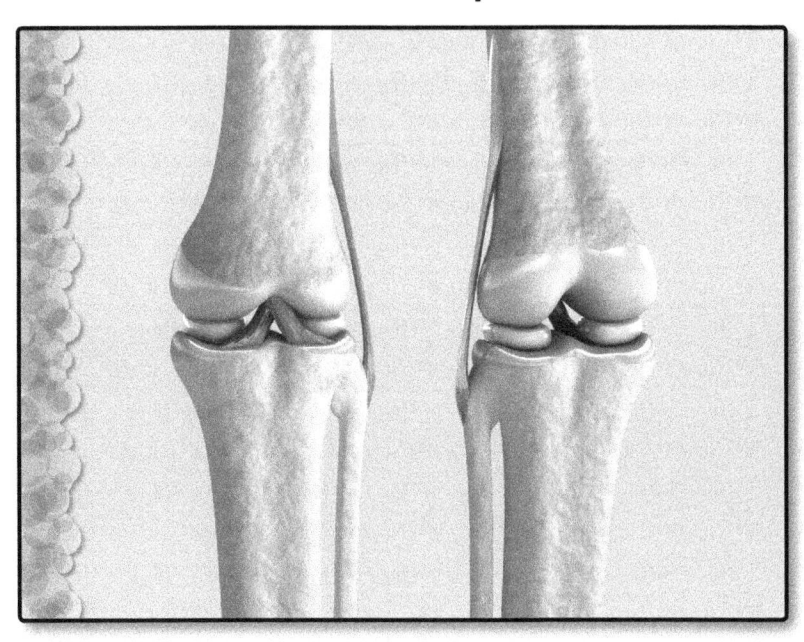

Assessment in primary science

In the primary science programme, assessment is a continuous, planned process that involves collecting information about student progress and learning in order to provide constructive feedback to students and parents, but also to inform planning and the next teaching steps.

Cambridge International Examinations Primary curriculum framework for science makes it clear what the students are expected to learn and achieve at each level. Our task as teachers is to make sure that we assess whether (or not) the students have achieved the stated goals using clearly-focused, varied, reliable and flexible methods of assessment.

In the Collins Primary Science course, assessment is continuous and in-built. It applies the principles of international best practice and ensures that assessment:

- is ongoing and regular
- supports individual achievement and allows for the students to reflect on their learning and set targets for themselves
- provides feedback and encouragement to the students
- allows for the integration of assessment into activities and classroom teaching by combining different assessment methods, including observations, questioning, self-assessment, formal and informal tasks
- uses strategies that cater for the variety of student needs in the classroom (language, physical, emotional and cultural), and acknowledges that the students do not all need to be assessed at the same time or in the same way
- allows for more formal summative assessment including controlled activities, tasks and class tests.

Assessing scientific enquiry skills

The development of scientific enquiry skills needs to be monitored. You need to check that the students acquire the basic skills as you teach and make sure that they are able to apply them in more complex activities and situations later on.

You can do this by identifying the assessment opportunities in different enquiry-based tasks and by asking appropriate informal assessment questions as the students work through and complete the tasks.

For example, the students may be involved in an activity where they are expected to plan and carry out a fair test investigating cars and ramps (*Plan investigative work:* Recognise that a test or comparison may be unfair).

As the students work through the activity you have the opportunity to assess whether they are able to identify:

- one thing that will change
- what things they will measure and record
- what things will be kept the same.

Once they have completed the task, you can ask some informal assessment questions, such as:

- Is a test the only way to do a scientific investigation? (*No, there are other methods of collecting and recording information, including using secondary sources.*)
- Is every test a fair test?
- Are there special things we need to do to make sure a test is fair?
- What should we do before we can carry out a fair test properly? (*Develop and write up a plan.*)
- Is a fair test in science the same as a written science or maths test at school?
- How is it different?

Assessment in primary science

Formal written assessment

The Collins Primary Science course offers a selection of Assessment Sheets that teachers can use to formally assess learning and to award marks if necessary. These sheets include questions posed in different ways, questions where the students fill in answers or draw diagrams and true or false questions among others.

Below are some examples of the types of questions, provided on the Assessment Sheets. The Assessment Sheets can be found at the back of this Teacher's Guide.

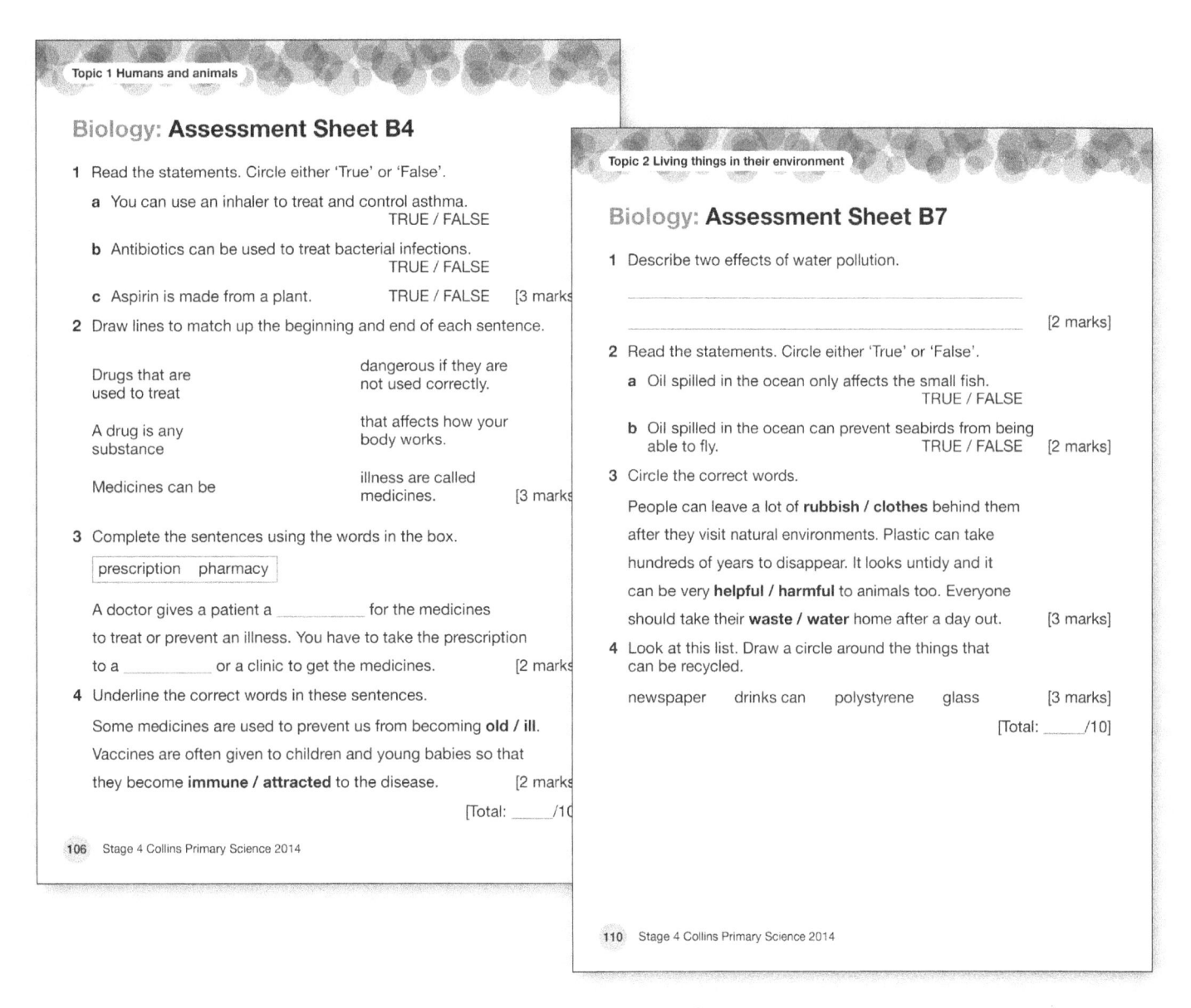

Topic 1 Humans and animals

Biology: Assessment Sheet B4

1 Read the statements. Circle either 'True' or 'False'.

  a You can use an inhaler to treat and control asthma.
                                                TRUE / FALSE
  b Antibiotics can be used to treat bacterial infections.
                                                TRUE / FALSE
  c Aspirin is made from a plant.   TRUE / FALSE   [3 marks]

2 Draw lines to match up the beginning and end of each sentence.

Drugs that are used to treat	dangerous if they are not used correctly.
A drug is any substance	that affects how your body works.
Medicines can be	illness are called medicines.

[3 marks]

3 Complete the sentences using the words in the box.

  prescription   pharmacy

  A doctor gives a patient a _____ for the medicines
  to treat or prevent an illness. You have to take the prescription
  to a _____ or a clinic to get the medicines.   [2 marks]

4 Underline the correct words in these sentences.
  Some medicines are used to prevent us from becoming **old / ill**.
  Vaccines are often given to children and young babies so that
  they become **immune / attracted** to the disease.   [2 marks]
                                                    [Total: ____/10]

106 Stage 4 Collins Primary Science 2014

Topic 2 Living things in their environment

Biology: Assessment Sheet B7

1 Describe two effects of water pollution.

  _____
  _____   [2 marks]

2 Read the statements. Circle either 'True' or 'False'.
  a Oil spilled in the ocean only affects the small fish.
                                                TRUE / FALSE
  b Oil spilled in the ocean can prevent seabirds from being
     able to fly.   TRUE / FALSE   [2 marks]

3 Circle the correct words.

  People can leave a lot of **rubbish / clothes** behind them
  after they visit natural environments. Plastic can take
  hundreds of years to disappear. It looks untidy and it
  can be very **helpful / harmful** to animals too. Everyone
  should take their **waste / water** home after a day out.   [3 marks]

4 Look at this list. Draw a circle around the things that can be recycled.

  newspaper   drinks can   polystyrene   glass   [3 marks]
                                                [Total: ____/10]

110 Stage 4 Collins Primary Science 2014

In addition to the materials supplied in the course, schools may opt for their students to take standardised Cambridge International Examinations progression tests at Stages 3, 4, 5 and 6. These tests are developed by Cambridge but they are written and marked in schools. Teachers download the tests and administer them in their own classrooms. Cambridge International Examinations provides a mark scheme and you can upload learners' test results and then analyse the results and create and print reports. You can also compare a learner's results against their class, school or other schools around the world and on a year-by-year basis.

xiii

Learning objectives matching grid

Stage 4 Biology Learning Objectives	Topic	Unit	Teacher's Guide pages
Humans and animals			
Know that humans (and some animals) have bony skeletons inside their bodies.	1	1	2
	1	2	4
	1	Consolidation	22
Know how skeletons grow as humans grow, support and protect the body.	1	1	2
	1	2	4
	1	3	6
	1	4	8
	1	5	10
	1	Consolidation	22
Know that animals with skeletons have muscles attached to the bones.	1	6	12
	1	Consolidation	22
Know how a muscle has to contract (shorten) to make a bone move and muscles act in pairs.	1	7	14
	1	8	16
	1	Consolidation	22
Explain the role of drugs as medicines.	1	9	18
	1	10	20
	1	Consolidation	22
Living things in their environment			
Investigate how different animals are found in different habitats and are suited to the environment in which they are found.	2	1	24
	2	2	26
	2	3	28
	2	Consolidation	38
Use simple identification keys.	2	4	30
	2	5	32
	2	Consolidation	38
Recognise ways that human activity affects the environment, e.g. river pollution, recycling waste.	2	6	34
	2	7	36
	2	Consolidation	38

Stage 4 Chemistry Learning Objectives	Topic	Unit	Teacher's Guide pages
States of matter			
Know that matter can be solid, liquid or gas.	3	1	40
	3	2	42
	3	Consolidation	52
Investigate how materials change when they are heated and cooled.	3	3	44
	3	4	46

Learning objectives matching grid

	3	5	48
	3	6	50
	3	Consolidation	52
Know that melting is when a solid turns into a liquid and is the reverse of freezing.	3	3	44
	3	4	46
	3	Consolidation	52
Observe how water turns into steam when it is heated but on cooling the steam turns back into water.	3	5	48
	3	6	50
	3	Consolidation	52

Stage 4 Physics Learning Objectives	Topic	Unit	Teacher's Guide pages
Sound			
Explore how sounds are made when objects, materials or air vibrate and learn to measure the volume of sound in decibels with a sound level meter.	4	1	54
	4	2	56
	4	6	64
	4	Consolidation	70
Investigate how sound travels through different materials to the ear.	4	3	58
	4	Consolidation	70
Investigate how some materials are effective in preventing sound from travelling through them.	4	4	60
	4	5	62
	4	Consolidation	70
Investigate the way pitch describes how high or low a sound is and that high and low sounds can be loud or soft. Secondary sources can be used.	4	7	66
	4	Consolidation	70
Explore how pitch can be changed in musical instruments in a range of ways.	4	8	68
	4	Consolidation	70
Electricity and magnetism			
Construct complete circuits using switch, cell (battery), wire and lamps.	5	1	72
	5	2	74
	5	Consolidation	88
Explore how an electrical device will not work if there is a break in the circuit.	5	3	76
	5	Consolidation	88
Know that electrical current flows and that models can describe this flow, e.g. particles travelling around a circuit.	5	4	78
	5	Consolidation	88
Explore the forces between magnets and know that magnets can attract or repel each other.	5	5	80
	5	6	82
	5	Consolidation	88
Know that magnets attract some metals but not others.	5	7	84
	5	8	86
	5	Consolidation	88

Scientific enquiry skills matching grid

Stage 4 Scientific enquiry skills	Topic	Unit	Teacher's Guide page
Ideas and evidence			
Collect evidence in a variety of contexts.	1	2	4
	1	3	6
	1	5	10
	1	6	12
	2	3	28
	2	7	36
	3	2	42
	4	1	54
	4	3	58
	4	4	60
	4	5	62
	4	6	64
	4	7	66
	4	8	68
	5	3	76
	5	5	80
	5	6	82
	5	7	84
	5	8	86
Test an idea or prediction based on scientific knowledge and understanding.	1	3	6
	3	1	40
	3	2	42
	3	5	48
	4	3	58
	4	4	60
	4	5	62
	4	6	64
	4	7	66
	4	8	68
	5	3	76
	5	6	82
	5	7	84
Plan investigative work			
Suggest questions that can be tested and make predictions; communicate these.	2	2	26
	3	1	40
	3	5	48
	4	2	56
	4	3	58
	4	4	60
	4	5	62
	5	5	80
	5	7	84

Stage 4 Scientific enquiry skills	Topic	Unit	Teacher's Guide page
Design a fair test and plan how to collect sufficient evidence.	1	4	8
	2	2	26
	3	3	44
	3	5	48
	4	2	56
	4	3	58
	4	4	60
	4	5	62
	5	3	76
	5	5	80
	5	7	84
Choose apparatus and decide what to measure.	1	4	8
	2	2	26
	2	3	28
	3	3	44
	3	5	48
	4	2	56
	4	3	58
	4	4	60
	4	5	62
	5	5	80
	5	7	84
Obtain and present evidence			
Make relevant observations and comparisons in a variety of contexts.	1	1	2
	1	2	4
	1	3	6
	1	5	10
	1	8	16
	1	9	18
	1	10	20
	2	1	24
	2	2	26
	2	3	28
	2	4	30
	2	5	32
	2	6	34
	2	7	36
	3	3	44
	3	4	46
	4	1	54
	4	7	66
	4	8	68
	5	1	72
	5	2	74
	5	3	76
	5	4	78
	5	7	84
	5	8	86

Scientific enquiry skills matching grid

Stage 4 Scientific enquiry skills	Topic	Unit	Teacher's Guide page
Measure temperature, time, force and length.	1	3	6
	2	2	26
	3	3	44
	3	4	46
Begin to think about the need for repeated measurements of, for example, length.	1	3	6
	1	10	20
	4	2	56
	4	4	60
	4	5	62
	5	5	80
Present results in drawings, bar charts and tables.	1	1	2
	1	3	6
	1	5	10
	1	8	16
	2	1	24
	2	3	28
	2	5	32
	3	3	44
	3	4	46
	4	1	54
	5	2	74
	5	7	84
	5	8	86
Consider evidence and approach			
Identify simple trends and patterns in results and suggest explanations for some of these.	1	7	14
	2	3	28
	3	1	40
	3	5	48
	3	6	50
	4	2	56
	4	7	66
	4	8	68
	5	2	74
	5	7	84
Explain what the evidence shows and whether it supports predictions. Communicate this clearly to others.	1	3	6
	2	2	26
	3	3	44
	3	4	46
	3	5	48
	3	6	50
	4	1	54
	4	3	58
	4	4	60
	4	5	62
	5	7	84

Stage 4 Scientific enquiry skills	Topic	Unit	Teacher's Guide page
Link evidence to scientific knowledge and understanding in some contexts.	1	7	14
	1	8	16
	1	10	20
	3	1	40
	3	3	44
	3	4	46
	3	6	50
	4	3	58
	4	4	60
	4	5	62
	5	2	74
	5	3	76
	5	7	84
	5	8	86

xvii

Lesson plans

Biology 2

Chemistry 40

Physics 54

Biology • Topic 1 Humans and animals

1.1 Animal skeletons

Student's Book pages 1–3

Biology learning objectives
- Know that humans (and some animals) have bony skeletons inside their bodies.
- Know that skeletons grow as humans grow, support and protect the body.

Resources
- Workbook pages 1 and 2
- Slideshow B1: Does it have a skeleton?

Classroom equipment
- large sheets of paper
- drawing or colouring equipment
- samples of X-rays, if possible
- reference books, pictures of different animals with their names

Scientific enquiry skills
- *Obtain and present evidence:* Make relevant observations and comparisons in a variety of contexts; present results in drawings, bar charts and tables.

Key words
- bones
- internal
- skeleton
- move
- support

> ⚠ Students should never touch animal bones that they find lying around in the environment. Bones can carry and spread quite serious diseases, including anthrax.

Scientific background

Animals can be classified as vertebrates (with backbones) and invertebrates (without backbones). The five groups of vertebrates are: fish, amphibians, reptiles, birds and mammals. (Humans are mammals, but students do not need to know the names of these groups at this stage.)

Invertebrates have no internal bone skeleton. They make up more than 98% of the world's animal species. Many invertebrates have a hydrostatic skeleton (a fluid-filled cavity surrounded by muscles). Others, such as insects and crustaceans, have a hard outer shell.

Skeletons are for movement, support and protection of internal organs and soft internal tissue such as nerves. Most vertebrate skeletons are made of bone but some, such as sharks', are made of cartilage. Weight for weight, bone is one of the strongest materials there is and it is light and flexible.

Introduction

- Before turning to the Student's Book, give each group a large sheet of paper. Ask the students to sketch their ideas of an animal with no skeleton. Once they have done this, explain that most animals have no bony skeleton inside them. Some, such as crabs, have hard outer shells. They need to shed their shells to grow. Ask: *What does the shell do for the animal?* (Supports it and protects it.) *When the shell is shed, the new shell under it is soft. What could happen to the animal while the shell is still soft?* (It could be eaten by a predator.) *Jellyfish and worms have a water skeleton, which is a water-filled space surrounded by muscles. Jellyfish are supported by the water they live in. What happens to a jellyfish out of water?* Refer to Student's Book page 2 and study the photograph with the class.

- Ask the class what they already know about bones and skeletons. Explain that they are going to draw a map of these ideas (a concept map). Ask them to write 'bones and skeletons' in a circle in the middle of a piece of paper. On the board, show the class how to develop the concept map. Write words for things that are related to bones and skeletons around the outside of the circle. Continue to add to the diagram, drawing lines to link new words to those already there. Let the students copy this class concept map. Some students could write a few words along the lines, to explain how the words are related. Ask each student to show their concept map to a partner and talk about it.

- Ask the students to look at page 1 of the Student's Book. Ask them to say what they are looking at. Discuss whether this skeleton came from a large or

Biology • Topic 1 Humans and animals 1.1

small animal. Ask questions such as: *What can you tell about this animal from its skeleton? What body parts can you recognise?*

Teaching and learning activities

- Ask the students to turn to pages 2 and 3 of the Student's Book. Emphasise that the frog, fish, snake and bird in the photographs have a bony internal skeleton, made up of lots of bones joined together, and a backbone. The skeleton helps the animal move and supports it, as well as protecting the soft parts inside its body (organs and tissues).
- Ask: *Which is the best type of skeleton for an animal to have to survive? Why do you think this?* Elicit that it depends on the animal's habitat, the way it needs to move and whether it is the prey of other animals.
- Show the class Slideshow B1. As you show each slide, ask them to say whether the animal has a skeleton and what type of skeleton it has.
- Let the students work in pairs or individually to complete Workbook page 1. They should think about what they have learned and what they saw in the slideshow.

Graded activities

1. The students can draw on the information in their books for some of the animals, but they may need to do some research of their own to find enough examples. If you have time, you could combine their answers to make a class table.

2. Encourage the students to find examples different from those used in their books and on the slideshow. Use reference books or the internet to find examples. For fun, you could expand this to look at 'superheroes' who have exoskeletons, such as Ironman, and discuss how having a bony internal skeleton combined with a hard shell is to their benefit.

3. Some students may be able to answer this question from their own experience, for example if they have ever broken a bone or had a dental X-ray. If you have samples of X-ray photographs, show them to the class. You may like to allow the students to discuss their experiences of having X-rays. Today, most X-rays are produced digitally and the doctor looks at the images on screen; images are seldom printed out.

Consolidate and review

- Show the class images of different animals. Let them sort these into groups according to whether they have a skeleton and what type of skeleton.
- Let the students complete Workbook page 2 as a consolidation task to remind them that some animals have bony skeletons and that you can normally work out what an animal is by looking at its skeleton. Ask more able students to label the body parts on each skeleton.

Differentiation

■ All of the students should be able to classify the animals they have studied in this lesson. They should be able to find other examples by doing some simple research. Students with a good general knowledge will be able to do the task from memory. Make sure the students do not include animals with exoskeletons in this task.

● Most of the students should be able to name locusts and beetles as they are mentioned in the text and they should make that association. Some students may have no experience of such animals and they will need to do some research. Make sure the students understand that a shell does not imply an exoskeleton; for instance, tortoises and turtles are vertebrates.

▲ Some of the students should be able to answer the questions with little or no help. More able students will delve deeper into the topic to find out how X-rays are produced and used.

Biology • Topic 1 Humans and animals 1.2

1.2 Your skeleton

Student's Book pages 4–5

Biology learning objectives
- Know that humans (and some animals) have bony skeletons inside their bodies.
- Know how skeletons grow as humans grow, support and protect the body.

Resources
- Workbook pages 3 and 4
- Slideshow B2: Bones
- DVD Activity B1: The skeleton

Classroom equipment
- large sheets of lining paper
- drawing and colouring equipment
- floppy rag doll
- model of human skeleton, if possible
- sterilised (boiled clean) chicken bones

Scientific enquiry skills
- *Ideas and evidence:* Collect evidence in a variety of contexts.
- *Obtain and present evidence:* Make relevant observations and comparisons in a variety of contexts.

Key words
- skeleton
- joints
- spine

> ⚠ Students should never touch animal bones that they find lying around in the environment. Bones can carry and spread quite serious diseases, including anthrax.

Scientific background

All vertebrates – fish, amphibians, reptiles, birds and mammals – contain an endoskeleton. This means that the bones are located inside the body. The skeleton is usually made from bone. Bones are hard, very strong, light and hollow. They are made in layers; the more layers there are in a bone, the stronger it is. Bones also have 'cement' between the layers, to provide more strength. Most bones contain a large amount of mineral substances, such as calcium and phosphorus. These minerals make the bone strong and hard.

Some bones do not contain as much of these substances and are known as spongy bone. This sort of bone is located where it can absorb knocks. The students do not need to know about the structure or composition of bones. This is not part of the Cambridge Primary Science Curriculum at this level and will not be tested in the Progression or Primary Checkpoint tests.

Bones have other very important functions: to manufacture red blood cells in the marrow, particularly in the femur or thigh bone; and to provide a point of attachment for the muscles. Tendons attach the muscles to the bones and are made from very strong, cord-like structures that do not stretch when they are pulled. Ligaments attach bone to bone at the point of a joint. Ligaments are very strong, fibre-like structures.

Introduction

- Ask for a volunteer to come to the front. Put two headings on the board: 'Having a skeleton' and 'Not having a skeleton'. Show the class the floppy rag doll and ask: *In what ways is this doll different from [volunteer student's name]?* Write the students' ideas and suggestions in the appropriate columns. Summarise their ideas by asking: *What advantages does having a skeleton give us?* The skeleton gives protection, support and allows us to move.
- Tell the students to work with a partner and to trace around each other's bodies on large sheets of lining paper. Then ask them to draw the bones they know about, inside the outline. When they have done this, ask the students to turn to Student's Book page 4 and look at the picture of the skeleton and let them compare it with what they have drawn.
- Point out and then ask individual students to come and identify: the skull, collarbone, breastbone, rib, spine (backbone), shoulder blade, hip bone, thigh bone, shinbone, kneecap, forearm and elbow.

Biology • Topic 1 Humans and animals 1.2

Teaching and learning activities

- Show the students images of bones in Slideshow B2. Point out that the bones are hard and there are movable joints between them. Ask: *What would we be like if we had no skeleton? In what ways would this affect us?* List their ideas on the board.

- If possible, examine some chicken bones. Encourage them to discuss with their partners some words to describe the bones. Ensure they identify that bones are hard, light and strong.

- Let the students complete Workbook page 3 independently to reinforce their knowledge of the names of different bones and their position in the human body. Observe them as they do so to see which students can name the bones easily.

- If you have time, ask the students to compare the human skeleton with those of different animals to say how they are similar and different. Use the skeletons in the Student's Book and the Workbook for this activity.

Graded activities

1 Encourage the students to choose three or four different bones and to compare these to say how they differ. Encourage them to consider size, shape, appearance and how they are joined to other bones.

2 Students who have broken bones in the past may be able to answer this question from experience. There are many different websites aimed at children where they can find the information. If possible, you could arrange for a healthcare worker to visit the class and tell the students about the different types of bone injuries.

3 Students will need to do some research to find out what to do when you have a cast and how to care for the cast. Then they will need to consider how best to present this information in a user-friendly way to educate young children.

Consolidate and review

- Show the class the slideshow again and let them make statements or ask questions about each slide.

- Use DVD Activity B1 to reinforce the names and location of different bones.

- Workbook page 4 can be used to check what the students have learned during this lesson. The joints activity will show you how well the students know the bones of the human skeleton. Allow them to use the diagram or a model if they need to.

- Ask the students to make a comic story showing what would happen if a) your bones did not grow as you grew, or b) your bones were soft and bendy.

Differentiation

■ All of the students should be able to say that bones differ in size and shape. They should be able to relate the shape of bones and way in which they are joined to their functions of support, movement and protection.

● Most of the students should be able to find out what happens when you break a bone. They should be able to find out about different kinds of fracture. More able students will be able to explain the differences clearly, possibly with the aid of diagrams.

▲ Some of the students should be able to develop a basic poster. They will present the information clearly and in a visually interesting way.

Biology • Topic **1** Humans and animals 1.3

1.3 Growing bones

Student's Book pages 6–7

Biology learning objective
- Know how skeletons grow as humans grow, support and protect the body.

Resources
- Workbook pages 5 and 6

Classroom equipment
- pens and pencils
- scrap paper
- rulers
- X-ray images, if available
- tape measures

Scientific enquiry skills
- *Ideas and evidence:* Collect evidence in a variety of contexts; test an idea or prediction based on scientific knowledge and understanding.
- *Obtain and present evidence:* Make relevant observations and comparisons in a variety of contexts; measure temperature, time, force and length; begin to think about the need for repeated measurements of, for example, length; present results in drawing, bar charts and tables.
- *Consider evidence and approach:* Explain what the evidence shows and whether it supports predictions. Communicate this clearly to others.

Key words
- X-ray
- cartilage
- bones
- calcium

Scientific background

In mammals, the skeleton starts to develop in the uterus. Growth does not occur at a steady rate; it is most rapid in the uterus. After birth, human growth is rapid in the first five years and then there are growth spurts at puberty and in the late teens. The skeleton continues to grow and change shape throughout life. This is most obvious in the structure of the jawbone. Human skeletons get smaller from their late twenties into old age. Students find these changes interesting, and investigating the relationship between the size of the skull, height and age offers opportunities for doing independent research and using ICT.

X-rays, such as the false coloured images shown in the Student's Book, allow us to 'see' bones through the skin and flesh. This is because the X-rays pass through the less dense tissues and affect a photographic film or electronic detector. Children's bones become bigger as they grow older, and some of the bones get closer together. More able students may be able to predict what happens after a person reaches 20 years of age; others may think that the bones continue to grow and this misconception should be addressed.

Introduction

- Remind the students that they have already discovered that all humans have a skeleton and that it is made up of bones. Look together at the X-rays of hands on page 6 of the Student's Book and discuss the opening paragraph. Then look together at the bones in the hand at different ages. If necessary, remind the students that X-rays show the bones through the skin. Tell them that darker colours indicate denser (thicker and stronger) bones and encourage them to find and examine the joints in each image. Ask the students to identify what they think is the main difference between the pictures. Ask them what happens to our bones as we become bigger.

- Have a class discussion based on the following questions: *Do all the students in this class have the same sized bones? Who would have the biggest and who would have the smallest bones in the school? Do some people grow more quickly than others? Who?*

Biology • Topic 1 Humans and animals 1.3

Teaching and learning activities

- Read through the information in the Student's Book and let the students discuss the answers to the questions.
- Let the students work in small groups to discuss and then write out neatly, on a sheet of paper, what they already know about bony skeletons. Let each group work in a different colour. After one minute, let the groups swap paper with another group. If they spot any mistakes they should correct them, but they should also add any facts they can to the other groups' work. Let them swap with a few other groups and then go through some of the ideas.
- Ask the question: *Do taller people have bigger bones than shorter people?* Let the students give their ideas and ask them to predict what they would find out if they investigated this. Decide as a class how this hypothesis could be tested. Pay careful attention to the need for standard measurements. Consider: units of length; where to measure to and from; the need for accurate measurements to the nearest cm/mm; the need to repeat measurements to give greater confidence in the results.
- Revise how to take measurements, using a tape measure if necessary. At this stage students should be able to measure and record lengths in either centimetres or millimetres, or a combination of these, although they may not be able to write measurements as decimals.

Graded activities

All students complete all three activities. Differentiation should be provided in the level of support students receive as they work, as well as by outcome (please see guidance in the 'Differentiation' box bottom right).

1 Try to place the students in groups of mixed heights for this investigation as that will give them a range of results. Before they start, discuss how they will take each measurement to make sure these are fair and accurate. For example, they should measure heights without shoes and standing straight against a wall.

2 If necessary, revise how to draw a bar chart to compare measurements. The students will need to decide how best to organise the data in the graphs. Make sure they refer to the graphs when they summarise their results.

3 Essentially this task is asking the students to extrapolate and to consider how the skeleton grows and changes over time. In five years' time the measurements would certainly be different, but the relationships between height and bone size would likely be similar. Students should also realise that people who are shorter than their friends now may be taller than their friends when they grow up.

Consolidate and review

- Talk through the investigation with the class. Ask them to share what they learned and the problems they encountered with the investigation. Compare results from different groups. Check whether the tallest and shortest students in the class have the biggest/smallest bones based on the data.
- Have a class discussion about how we know that bones grow as we grow. Possible answers include that we can see and measure them on X-rays, but also that we can feel and measure them on the body. Similarly, if bones did not grow, our limbs would be floppy as the skin and muscles would be larger than the bones.
- Ask students to work in pairs to produce a multiple choice or true and false test about skeletons. They should include at least five questions. Let the pairs exchange tests, complete each others' and then mark their own work.

Differentiation

■ All of the students should be able to take measurements and record them in a table. Observe the groups as they are doing this investigation to make sure that everyone takes part. Students who struggle with exact millimetre measurements can work to the closest centimetre.

● Most of the students should be able to draw bar graphs by this stage. Assist those who struggle by asking them leading questions and, if necessary, referring them back to their maths books to see how this is done. More able students will be able to draw sensible conclusions based on the graphs and refer to the graphs to make their points.

▲ Some of the students should realise that the measurements will change. They should give cohesive reasons for this and also suggest that the proportions are likely to remain similar.

Biology • Topic 1 Humans and animals 1.4

1.4 Functions of the skeleton

Student's Book pages 8–9

Biology learning objective
- Know how skeletons grow as humans grow, support and protect the body.

Resources
- Workbook pages 7 and 8
- Slideshow B2: Bones

Classroom equipment
- A3 and A4 paper
- sticky tape
- scissors
- paperclip and assorted weights
- reference books or access to the internet for research
- model of human skeleton, if available
- cotton reels and string, or cardboard tubes or straws cut into sections

Scientific enquiry skills
- *Plan investigative work:* Design a fair test and plan how to collect sufficient evidence; choose apparatus and decide what to measure.

Key words
- support
- protect
- organs
- backbone

> ⚠ Make sure the students work carefully when they are cutting and sticking paper. Use scissors rather than craft knives for activities such as this.

Scientific background

The skeleton is important because it serves three main purposes: it protects the soft inner organs of the body, it supports the body, and it aids movement.

The skeleton protects the organs, for example the ribs protect the lungs. It allows us to move because it has joints and supports our body, for example the spine keeps us upright.

The spine is not a single bone; it is made of 26 smaller bones called vertebrae. The vertebrae are separated by small disks of spongy cartilage, which prevent the bones from rubbing together and act as a natural shock absorber. These disks absorb shocks when you jump or make other strong movements using the bones in the legs.

The spine is crucial in terms of supporting the frame and also in terms of protecting the spinal cord and nerve pathways from the body to the brain. It is the spine that allows the body to twist and bend, and holds the frame upright.

Introduction

- Show the class Slideshow B2 again and ask students to try to name the bones and parts of the body as you show the slides.
- Spend some time focusing on the bones themselves, what they look like and how they are structured. Ask the students if they know what makes the long bones (thigh, shin and arm bones) so strong. (They are hard and layered but hollow, which is what makes them light and strong.)

Teaching and learning activities

- Turn to Student's Book pages 8 and 9. Encourage the students to feel their spines and to say what they can feel. They need to realise that the 'bumps' they can feel are separate bones. Look at the diagram of the spine. Use the cotton reels or sections of tube to show how vertebrae are found on top of each other. If you place a stick through the middle, the students can see that it is possible to twist and turn these bones but not to bend them, like an elbow or knee.

Biology • Topic 1 Humans and animals 1.4

- Use some of the animal skeleton pictures from earlier in this topic to compare the backbones of different animals. Humans are the only mammals that walk upright all the time (monkeys and apes also have semi-vertical spines, but they do not walk upright all the time).

- Divide the students into groups of three and explain that they are going to create model bones. Give each student in the group a role (timekeeper, spokesperson and manager). Explain that their task is to make a model of a bone from paper. They are to make the bone as strong as possible. Ask the students to put their hands up if they have an idea about how to test the strength of their model bone, for example by hanging weights from the middle.

Graded activities

All students complete all three activities. Differentiation should be provided in the level of support students receive as they work, as well as by outcome (please see guidance in the 'Differentiation' box opposite).

1 Provide groups with paper (A3 and A4), paperclips and sticky tape. Remind the students about the structure of the bones they looked at in the last activity. Explain that bone is made of layers of material that make it very light but strong. Let the groups work for a set time to make their model thigh bones. The students should roll the paper up to make the bones. Some may make solid bones and some may make hollow bones. Hollow objects are lighter than solid objects but can be very strong. Ask the students to make a record of their investigation. They should draw their model and describe how they made it on pages 7 and 8 of the Workbook.

2 Ask each group to present their model thigh bone to the class. Let them hang weights from the centre while holding the model at either end or clamping it into stands. The winning group is the one with the strongest bone model. Ask the students: *What made some models stronger than others?* The students should then explain why the strongest model worked so well. Go round the groups and ask them how well their investigation went and how effectively they worked together as groups.

3 Let the students use the model or slideshow to look at the backbone in more detail if they prefer. Students have to draw their model, but you can allow them to build it if you have time. Cotton reels, sections of tube or straw and even hollow pasta can be used to model vertebrae.

Consolidate and review

- Ask the students to work in pairs to make a list of vocabulary relevant to skeletons (for example, bones, joints, movement, support). Encourage them to think back over the past few lessons.

- As a class, make a complete list of the suggestions, where appropriate asking the students their reasons for a word's inclusion in the list. Display the list prominently.

- Tell the students to look at the written notes they made earlier in Unit 1.3 and to notice how much more they now know. Allow them to add any new information they have learned.

Differentiation

■ All of the students should be able to draw a diagram of the model and write a sentence to say how they made it.

● Most of the students should be able to comment on how they made their bones strong. Some of the students should be able to say what made other groups' models stronger, if they were, and evaluate how well they worked as a group.

▲ Some of the students will be able to apply their knowledge and think creatively and critically about the structure and function of the spine and use this understanding to design an appropriate model.

Biology • Topic 1 Humans and animals 1.5

1.5 Protecting your organs

Student's Book pages 10–11

Biology learning objective
- Know how skeletons grow as humans grow, support and protect the body.

Resources
- Workbook page 9
- Slideshow B3: Protective sports equipment

Classroom equipment
- paper and drawing equipment
- digital cameras
- examples of protective sports equipment, if possible (helmets, cricket pads, safety glasses)
- model of human skeleton, if possible

Scientific enquiry skills
- *Ideas and evidence:* Collect evidence in a variety of contexts.
- *Obtain and present evidence:* Make relevant observations and comparisons in a variety of contexts; present results in drawings, bar charts and tables.

Key words
- skull
- ribs
- ribcage

Scientific background

Besides the spine, the skull and ribcage are important in terms of protecting vulnerable and important organs.

The skull basically acts like a 'crash helmet' to protect the brain and the soft facial organs (eyes and tongue). The skull is actually made up of different bones. The bones at the top and back of the skull protect the brain, while the front of the skull is made of facial bones that protect the eyes and tongue. Human babies are born with spaces between the bones in their skulls. This allows the bones to move, close up and even overlap as the baby is born and moves through the birth canal. As babies grow, the spaces between the bones slowly close up, and immovable joints called sutures are formed between the different parts of the skull.

The ribcage has two important functions: protection and support. It protects the heart, lungs and liver, and provides a frame for the muscles of the upper body. In addition, the ribcage is flexible and can expand and contract as we breathe.

The ribcage is made up of the sternum, 12 vertebrae and 12 pairs of rib bones. The sternum, or breastbone, is a flat bone at the front of the chest. The rib bones are attached at the back to the vertebrae and the top seven pairs are attached to the sternum (by cartilage) at the front.

Introduction

- Remind the students that our skeleton keeps our body upright (supports us) and allows us to move. Ask them to suggest what other functions it has (it protects the organs inside our body). Spend some time discussing why our insides need protection (the organs are soft and easily damaged).
- Ask the class where their brains are located (inside their head/skull). Spend some time discussing why the brain is important (without going into too much detail about the nervous system). Students should realise that the brain is a really important organ as it controls all our body functions.
- Let the students feel their own (or each other's) skulls and describe what they feel.
- Ask the students to feel and count their ribs and locate any other bones that can be felt from the surface. Ask: *How many ribs can you count? What do they feel like? Do they move? Why are they there?*

Biology • Topic 1 Humans and animals 1.5

Teaching and learning activities

- Turn to Student's Book pages 10 and 11. Study the diagrams, then read through the text with the students and get them to answer the questions orally as a class.
- Explain that our bones are strong and that they are designed to protect us during normal activities, but that they can be damaged by impact, accident or extreme sports. For example, motorcyclists wear helmets to protect their skulls in case of an accident; cricket players wear pads and face masks because a fast, hard cricket ball can damage bone.
- Show the class Slideshow B3. Discuss what equipment each player is wearing and what bones and/or body parts are being protected.

Graded activities

1 Let the students work in groups to compile a list of sports before asking them to turn to Workbook page 9 to record their information in the table.

2 Allow the students to work on their own or in pairs to complete this activity. If they cannot draw or photograph the equipment, they should look for pictures in newspapers or magazines.

3 Provide the students with equipment to make a poster or brochure. Encourage them to think carefully about why children should wear helmets in different situations and then to consider appropriate ways to encourage them to do so.

Consolidate and review

- Let the students present the pieces of sports equipment they have chosen to the class. Allow other students to ask questions about the presentations. Ask the students: *What injuries might a sportsperson get if they did not wear this equipment?*
- Let the students make a summary concept map around the topic, titled 'Functions of our bones'. Check their maps to make sure they include: provide a frame; support; movement; protection of soft body parts.
- Choose one or two activities that the class has not considered (e.g. horse riding, water skiing, mountain climbing, ice-skating, motor racing and so on). Let the students discuss what the potential risks are in each activity and then suggest what they can do to protect the bones.

Differentiation

■ All of the students should be able to make a list of sports in which the participants wear protective gear. They should be able to add some examples beyond the slideshow. Some students may struggle to name the equipment correctly. If this is the case, let them do some research to source the information they need.

● Most of the students should be able to provide at least a simple explanation of how the equipment they have chosen protects the body. More able students will be able to provide detailed and well-structured explanations using the correct scientific vocabulary for body parts.

▲ Some of the students should be able to identify the need to wear a helmet while cycling, skateboarding or riding a scooter. They will find creative and practical ways of encouraging young children to do so.

Biology • Topic 1 Humans and animals 1.6

1.6 Muscles

Student's Book pages 12–13

Biology learning objective

- Know that animals with skeletons have muscles attached to the bones.

Resources

- Workbook page 10
- Image B1: Ligaments and tendons

Classroom equipment

- large sheets of paper
- drawing equipment
- a chicken (or turkey) leg and thigh with meat (muscle) attached, if available

Scientific enquiry skills

- *Ideas and evidence:* Collect evidence in a variety of contexts.

Key words
- muscles
- tendons

⚠️ If you are using raw chicken in the classroom, do not let the students handle it. Use gloves yourself when you handle it, wash your hands and any containers afterwards, and do not cook or eat chicken that has been used in this way as it could cause food poisoning. Keep this sample for the next lesson by refrigerating it until you need it.

Scientific background

There are different kinds of muscle in the body. The most commonly known are the skeletal muscles, such as the extensor and flexor muscles in the upper arm – the biceps and the triceps. (Students can feel these muscles if they flex their arms.) Antagonistic muscles always work in pairs; as muscles work by contracting, they need the opposite muscle to contract in order to return to the original position.

Some muscles have very specialised jobs to do, such as the cardiac muscle found in the heart wall. Cardiac muscle contracts, on average, 70 times a minute throughout a person's lifetime.

Muscles require both oxygen and a food supply to function normally. Muscle contraction produces waste products, including carbon dioxide, that need to be removed. The delivery of oxygen and nutrients and the removal of waste are achieved through the blood supply. Exercise not only increases muscle mass, it also increases muscle efficiency. Inactivity leads to muscle wasting, which can be seen when a limb has been in a plaster cast for some time.

Introduction

- Let the students feel their upper arms as they bend and flex their elbows. Ask: *Are you feeling bone? What do you think you are feeling?* Introduce the term 'muscle'.

- Having spent some time looking at bones the students will have a clear idea that we have a skeleton for three purposes: protection, support and movement. In this lesson, the students are going to learn how the muscles that cover the skeleton work to allow movement. Introduce the idea by asking the class whether bones can move on their own. Try to elicit the idea that we need muscles to move.

- Show the students an uncooked chicken leg that has had the skin removed. (Turkey would be even better, as it is bigger.) Discuss what the muscle looks like. Explain that meat is really the muscle of animals. Flex the leg so that they can see the muscles move. Cut away some of the muscle to show how the tendons attach the muscles to the bones. Examine the tendons and compare them with the muscle (they are much harder and stronger and they are not as flexible).

- Show the class Image B1 of tendons and ligaments so they can see where these occur in the human skeleton. Explain that tendons connect muscles bones, and ligaments connect bones to bones.

Biology • Topic 1   Humans and animals 1.6

Teaching and learning activities

- Turn to Student's Book pages 12 and 13. Read the information and study the diagrams. Discuss the questions as a class, making sure the students know that we need muscles to move our bones (the actual mechanism of movement is covered in Unit 1.7). Use common names for muscles at this stage – students do not need to know scientific terms, nor do they need to memorise types of muscle. Discuss the answers as a class and sort out any misconceptions.

- Read through the muscle facts with the class. If they are interested, let them do some research to find other 'Did you know?' type facts about muscles. One fact the students might find interesting is the well-known saying: 'It takes 17 muscles to smile and 43 muscles to frown'. Let them smile and frown while looking in a mirror and feeling their faces move. Other interesting facts are: we have over 600 muscles; 40% of our body mass is muscle; we use 200 muscles to take one step.

Graded activities

1 Provide each student with a sheet of paper and let them draw their own (or their partner's) outline and then label the given muscles. Allow them to add more labels (in a different colour) if they know more muscles.

2 Students can find this information in a dictionary or other reference book, or by using the internet. Encourage them to think about more than just the function of each and to consider their structure as well.

3 Students will need to do some research to find out what muscles need and how to build and maintain muscles.

Consolidate and review

- Use Workbook page 10 to consolidate the work done on muscles in this unit.

- Ask the students to imagine they are a muscle in an animal's body. Let them say what muscle they are and then ask them to describe their day, perhaps complaining about how hard they work. Alternatively, let the students role play an argument between two muscles about who works the hardest. You can allocate different muscles to different students to prevent arguments.

Differentiation

■ All of the students should be able to draw an outline of the body and correctly label the muscle groups given. More able students will be able to add some other muscles and may know the names of some muscle groups.

● Most of the students should be able to give a basic answer to this question. More able students will give more coherent and detailed explanations, perhaps with diagrams.

▲ Some of the students should be able to find out that muscles need fuel (food), water and exercise. They will be able to present more detailed and varied programmes for keeping muscles healthy.

13

Biology • Topic 1 Humans and animals 1.7

1.7 Moving your bones

Student's Book pages 14–15

Biology learning objective
- Know how a muscle has to contract (shorten) to make a bone move and muscles act in pairs.

Resources
- Workbook page 11
- PCM B1: Model arm muscle (make this in advance)

Classroom equipment
- drawing equipment
- exercise mats
- chicken (or turkey) thigh and leg from previous lesson (refrigerated to keep it fresh)

Scientific enquiry skills
- *Consider evidence and approach:* Identify simple trends and patterns in results and suggest explanations for some of these; link evidence to scientific knowledge and understanding in some contexts.

Key words
- **muscles**   • **contract**   • **relax**

> ⚠️ If you are using raw chicken in the classroom, do not let the students handle it. Use gloves yourself when you handle it, wash your hands and any containers afterwards, and do not cook or eat chicken that has been used in this way as it could cause food poisoning.

Scientific background

An internal skeleton is made up of a system of levers, which are moved by the contraction of muscles attached to bones. Muscles cause movement of bones at joints. Muscles are attached to bones by tendons. When muscles contract (pull) they get shorter and fatter, and they pull the bone. Muscles can only pull, not push. When the muscle relaxes, it gets longer and thinner and the bone moves away. Muscles work in antagonistic pairs – when one contracts the other relaxes. Some muscles move involuntarily, without us controlling this movement; this happens in the heart, eye, gut, stomach and between the ribs.

Students should understand that hands and faces have many small muscles, which enable them to undertake very complex activities such as writing and speaking.

Introduction

- Ask the students to stand up and then sit down. Ask them to describe what was happening when they did this. Which parts of the body were involved? Explain that today they will be finding out how the muscles work to make their bodies move. Ask the students to give examples of how their bodies move and make a list of them. Ask: *Can you bend your arm? Lift your leg? Wiggle your toes?*

- Use the chicken leg to revise the concept of a muscle and how muscles are attached to the bones by tendons. Point out that there are many different muscles in the leg and that they always occur in pairs – as one muscle contracts (gets shorter) the other relaxes (gets longer) enabling movement to take place. In order for the bones to return to their original position, the opposite muscle must contract to pull the bones back into place.

Teaching and learning activities

- Show a paper model of an arm muscle (made previously, from PCM B1) to demonstrate how the muscle gets shorter and fatter as it contracts and longer and thinner as it relaxes.

- Tell the students that one of the muscles pulls the arm in one direction while the other muscle pulls the other way. Neither of the muscles pushes the arm. Stress that muscles can only pull.

- Ask the students to look at the pictures on pages 14 and 15 of the Student's Book. Get them to read through the information while they feel their own arm muscles as they move their arms. Ask: *Which muscle is pulling each time?* The Student's Book gives a simple explanation of how we move our arms.

Biology • Topic 1 Humans and animals 1.7

- You could take the students to the gym or out on the grass for this short series of exercises. Provide mats for them to lie on. Tell the students to lie flat on their backs on the ground and feel their stomachs while raising their legs. Ask them to describe what is happening to their stomach muscles. Discuss with the class how muscles move bones by pulling on them and that muscles become short and fat when they do so. Ask the students to try different movements, such as walking on toes, lifting objects, doing press-ups, standing on hands and doing knee bends, to feel and see muscles and joints working.
- Back in the classroom, explain that some muscles, such as the heart muscle and rib muscles, move involuntarily. Remind the students that tendons attach muscles to the bones. Ask the students: *What happens if a tendon is torn?* (You cannot move the joint.)

Graded activities

1 Students should work on their own to complete this activity. They should use colour and they can refer to the model muscle to make their drawings.

2 Let students work in pairs to complete the activity. Let them take turns to do an action and give an explanation.

3 Students should complete this activity on their own.

Consolidate and review

- Let the students work in groups to review and summarise what they have learned about muscles and movement. Give some groups a chance to present their work to the class.
- Let the students complete Workbook page 11. Check their work to make sure they understand how muscles work in pairs to allow movement.

Differentiation

■ All of the students should be able to draw a shortened, fattened muscle. More able students will provide more accurate drawings of the striated structure of muscle fibres.

● Most of the students should be able to point to, if not name, the relevant muscles. Observe students as they do this activity to make sure that they can identify which muscles are contracting and which are relaxing.

▲ Some of the students should be able to explain that bones cannot move without muscles. They will be able to explain the process clearly and write a coherent paragraph with a main idea and supporting facts.

Biology • Topic 1 Humans and animals 1.8

1.8 Investigate moving bones

Student's Book pages 16–17

Biology learning objective
- Know how a muscle has to contract (shorten) to make a bone move and muscles act in pairs.

Classroom equipment
- card, paper fasteners and elastic bands for each group
- drawing equipment
- reference books

Scientific enquiry skills
- *Obtain and present evidence:* Make relevant observations and comparisons in a variety of contexts; present results in drawings, bar charts and tables.
- *Consider evidence and approach:* Link evidence to scientific knowledge and understanding in some contexts.

Key words
- model
- muscles

> ⚠ Students need to be supervised when working with push-pin paper fasteners as the points are sharp and it is easy for them to hurt themselves if they push them through the card carelessly. Remind them that elastic bands snap back when stretched, so they need to attach them carefully to the model.

Scientific background

There is no new scientific content in this unit. The students will need to consolidate and apply what they already know about joints, bones and muscles to build a model to demonstrate how a pair of antagonistic muscles works together to allow for movement at a joint. The model shows a hinge joint, such as the ones found at the elbow and knee; however, all movement at joints happens as a result of muscle pairs like this.

Introduction

- Explain to the students that they are going to work in pairs to make a model that will help them to understand how muscles work in pairs to create movement. Turn to Student's Book page 16 and discuss question 1. Make sure the students can explain what a model is and how it can help them to demonstrate scientific concepts.

Teaching and learning activities

- Refer the students to the instructions and diagram in the Student's Book (pages 16 and 17). Give each pair two pieces of stiff card, and ask them to join these at one end using paper fasteners (if time is short, these could be prepared beforehand). Tell the students to push four more brass fasteners through the card as shown. Give each pair two rubber bands, each of which should be attached to the brass fasteners.

- Discuss the questions about the model as the students complete their models. Explain to the students that the two lengths of card represent the bones in their arm and that they need to attach the rubber bands to help the arm move. These bands represent the muscles. Give students help where needed to allow them to complete the task.

- Ask the students to explore what happens to the two 'muscles' as the 'arm' is moved.

Biology • Topic 1   Humans and animals 1.8

Graded activities

1 Students can use their models as a guide, but they should work on their own to draw their diagrams and label them.

2 Let the students complete this task orally in pairs. Have a class feedback session to share their ideas.

3 Students can do research on the internet or using reference books to find out about different types of involuntary muscles and where these are found in our bodies. They should then draw their own conclusions about why it is important that these muscles work on their own.

Consolidate and review

- Demonstrate how the model relates to the movement of the human arm. One of the muscles pulls the arm in one direction, while the other muscle pulls the other way. Neither of the muscles pushes the arm. Ask the students to feel their own arm muscles again as they move their arms, and ask them which muscle is pulling each time. Explain to the students that although this is basically how limbs are moved, the model is not perfect because muscles do not stretch in quite the same way as a rubber band. The reality is also more complicated because of the number of muscles involved. Ask them to look at the illustration of the human muscle system on page 12 of the Student's Book, and to notice the number of muscles and where they are attached. Finally, ask the students to feel their faces as they smile, frown and wrinkle their noses. Ask them to think of the number of muscles involved in these processes.

- Discuss some of the difficulties people might have if skeletal muscle was involuntary. If you have time, do some research into muscle disorders and let the students discuss what they find out.

Differentiation

■ All of the students should be able to draw and label the model. If they struggle with drawing, allow them to photograph the model and then label the photograph.

● Most of the students should be able to work out that the knee bends in the opposite direction to the elbow, so although you could use this model, you would need to reconsider what the parts represent and how you would position the model.

▲ Some of the students should be able to find out what involuntary muscles are. They will be able to give several examples and to explain the importance of these muscles being involuntary.

Biology • Topic 1 Humans and animals 1.9

1.9 Drugs and medicines

Student's Book pages 18–19

Biology learning objective
- Explain the role of drugs as medicines.

Resources
- Workbook page 12
- Slideshow B4: Medicines

Classroom equipment
- samples of packaging from over-the-counter medicines
- posters about drug/medicine safety and use from local health authorities, if available
- piece of card about 5 cm x 5 cm for each student

Scientific enquiry skills
- *Obtain and present evidence:* Make relevant observations and comparisons in a variety of contexts.

Key words
- drugs
- medicines
- prescription
- pharmacy

⚠ Never use real medicines to show the students, and discourage them from showing their own medication to peers unless you are supervising them. Students with inhalers, for example, should never allow other students to try these out.

Scientific background

Humans have life processes (like other animals), which are maintained by organ systems. Any substance that alters the way in which our bodies work is a drug.

The concept of drugs and/or medicine is not a modern one. In ancient cultures, healers used plant extracts to soothe and relieve aches and pains. The students will learn more about this in the next unit.

The students should be taught never to take prescription medicines unless told to by a doctor. They need to know that some people take prescription drugs regularly to stay alive but that the effects of some drugs can be fatal when taken by healthy people. The students should be taught that all drugs are potentially dangerous.

Be aware that in some communities, the word medicine may be less familiar than the word drug. Where American English is the norm, a pharmacy may be called a drug store, and people will talk about drugs rather than medicines.

Introduction

- Invite a health professional, such as the school nurse or an advisor from the local health department or clinic, to help in this lesson. If this is not possible, take the role yourself. Place the students in a large circle. Ensure that each student has a pencil or pen and give them each a piece of card about 5 cm x 5 cm. Ask them to write down the name of a drug and then pass their card to the person on their right. Ask each student in turn to read the name of the drug on the card they now have. After each one, agree with the class whether or not the substance is a drug. There will be some duplicates.

- Ask the health professional to explain what a drug is in scientific terms. Encourage the students to ask questions or give them all another piece of card and ask them to write down their question and then pass it to the student on their left. Ask the students to read the question they now have. With the health professional, answer the questions.

- Show the students a collection of packaging, some from drugs and some not, such as aspirin, cough mixture, coffee (decaffeinated and with caffeine), cola (decaffeinated and with caffeine). Ask the students to decide which ones are drugs and which ones are not (most are drugs as they affect the way the body behaves).

- Discuss prescriptions with the class. Make sure they understand that this is an instruction from a doctor and that some medicines are only supplied on prescription and can only be purchased from a pharmacy.

Biology • Topic 1 Humans and animals 1.9

Teaching and learning activities

- Some students in the class will be used to taking medicines in order to keep healthy, so this next section of work may need sensitive handling. Ask the class to share their own definitions by asking: *What is a drug?* Explain that this is an all-embracing term used to describe any substance that changes the way the body functions. When drugs are used as medicines, these changes are beneficial, such as in opening up the air passages when an asthmatic uses an inhaler, or taking a cough medicine when we have a cold. Point out that the term 'drug' tends to be used in a detrimental way to describe a substance that is taken illegally.
- Show the class Slideshow B4 and let them say what the different slides show and how each of these medicines is used.
- Look together at Student's Book pages 18 and 19 and, after answering question 1, ask: *What effects do you think these medicines might have on the body? What are side effects?* Explain that side effects are unwanted effects, such as headaches, weight gain, nausea, which can be produced when a person takes a drug. This is true of beneficial drugs/medicines – the instructions given on the labels must be followed carefully to reduce possible side effects. Discuss question 2 as a class.
- Look at the instructions and information on any (empty) medicine containers you have brought to class. Compare these to find out what sort of information is common to most medicine packaging.

Graded activities

1 If you wish to vary this activity, you could give each group a different box from real medication. If this is not possible, all the groups can use the sample label on page 19 of the Student's Book.

2 This activity relates to the label in the book, so students must use this to answer the question. To do this, they need to read and understand the information and then draw their own conclusions based on this.

3 Students should work in groups to complete this task. Allow them to refer to publications from local health authorities and to do some of their own research to find out about the dangers of and safety precautions for storing medicines.

Consolidate and review

- Organise the class into small groups. Present each group with a set of jumbled-up cards with a word from the following sentence on each: *All medicines are drugs but not all drugs are medicines.* Ask the groups to rearrange the words to make an accurate sentence.
- Ask the students to share any experiences of taking medicines, for example prescriptions from the doctors when they have been ill. Explain that if any medicine is misused and the dosage instructions are not followed it can cause harm.
- Let the students complete Workbook page 12 independently.

Differentiation

■ All of the students should be able to read the information label in the book, but some may struggle with real-life packaging as the language is more complex. They should be able to explain why the information is given and why it is important.

● Most of the students will be able to critically read the information and advise Mrs Smith to consult a pharmacist or doctor before she decides to take the tablets.

▲ Some of the students should be able to draw up some basic instructions for the safe storage of medicines. More able students will consider the issue more comprehensively and draw up a detailed list with clear instructions and reasons for these.

19

Biology • Topic 1 Humans and animals 1.10

1.10 Different medicines

Student's Book pages 20–21

Biology learning objective
- Explain the role of drugs as medicines.

Resources
- Workbook page 13
- PCM B2: Aloe vera
- PCM B3: Medicines wordsearch
- Slideshow B4: Medicines

Classroom equipment
- samples of packaging from over-the-counter medicines

Scientific enquiry skills
- *Obtain and present evidence:* Make relevant observations and comparisons in a variety of contexts; begin to think about the need for repeated measurements of, for example, length.
- *Consider evidence and approach:* Link evidence to scientific knowledge and understanding in some contexts.

Key words
- **moisturiser**
- **aspirin**
- **vaccine**
- **immune**

> ⚠️ Never use real medicines to show the students, and discourage them from showing their own medication to peers unless you are supervising them. Students with inhalers, for example, should never allow other students to try these out.

Scientific background

Any substance that alters the way in which our bodies work is a drug.

The concept of drugs and/or medicine is not a modern one. In ancient cultures, healers used plant extracts to soothe and relieve aches and pains. Many of the plants that were discovered by ancient cultures are still used today. The leaves of willows, which contain a compound very similar to aspirin, were chewed by Native Americans to relieve aches and pains. A major treatment in heart disease is digitalis, found in foxgloves. The cinchona tree, found in South America, gives us quinine from its bark to fight malaria. Many other plants have proven invaluable as sources of vitamins, which are vital to growth and proper development.

Introduction

- Show the class Slideshow B4 again. Remind the students that some of these medicines are freely available from pharmacies or large stores (this will depend on where you live and which shops sell over-the-counter medicines), while others are only available if you go to a clinic or doctor and get a prescription.
- Remind the students that some drugs are not medicines and that their use is against the law.

Teaching and learning activities

- Turn to Student's Book pages 20 and 21. Read through the information and answer the questions as a class.
- Ask the students if they can think of any traditional medicines that are used in their community or country. (You may want to introduce the terms 'herbal medicines' or 'complimentary medicines'.) Explain that although many medicines we use are not harmful to us, they are also not scientifically proven to work. Open this up into a class discussion about the types of questions a scientist might need to ask in order to test if a medicine works. The students should know that the tests need to be safe and fair, and that scientists repeat tests many times to make sure the results are accurate.
- If you feel it is appropriate at this point, you could discuss illegal drugs with the students, but there is no need to go into this aspect of the topic in great detail. Students simply need to know that some drugs are harmful and addictive and that selling or buying them is against the law. If drug abuse is a problem in your community, you may like to have some posters or leaflets available about where to get help if individuals or their family members have a drug problem.

Biology • Topic 1 Humans and animals 1.10

- Ask the students if they have ever had a vaccination. There may be some local vaccination programs in your area that you could refer to. Ask how the vaccine was given; was it by injection or taken orally? Explain to the students that a vaccine is a 'preventative medicine'; it is given to prevent you getting a particular disease or illness. When you have a particular vaccine you build up resistance to the disease and become immune to it, so you cannot catch it and become ill.

Graded activities

1. Students can work in pairs or small groups to sort the samples of empty medicine packaging into two groups: those that go on the outside of the body and those that go inside the body. Stress to the students the importance of reading the instructions on the packets to make sure the medicine is used correctly.

2. Students should use PCM B2 to prepare a fact sheet about Aloe vera. They should use the information on the PCM to suggest arguments for and against its use as a medicine. Their conclusion is likely to be that as Aloe vera is safe to use, then people may as well continue to use it as a medicine.

3. Students should do some research, using books or the internet, to find out about two more plants used in medicine. They should record their findings on page 13 of their Workbook.

Consolidate and review

- Let the students present their fact sheets from the activity to each other in small groups. Let them ask each other questions and give feedback about how clear their presentations are.

- Ask the students to make a concept map around the topic of drugs and medicines. Display the completed charts in the classroom for comment.

- Use the wordsearch on PCM B3 as a fun way to check that the students have developed the vocabulary needed to talk about drugs as medicine. Give them time to exchange the completed wordsearches and to try to find each other's words.

Differentiation

■ All of the students should be able to sort the medicine packages into two groups with little or no help. Some students may need help with reading the information on the packaging.

● Most of the students should be able to prepare a basic fact sheet. However, some students will provide more information and clear arguments for and against the use of Aloe vera as a medicine, based on their research or experience.

▲ Some of the students should be able to undertake individual research with little or no support. They will be able to locate relevant information and complete the activity in the workbook. Some students will need additional support to find the information. Students who are less able English speakers will find this activity challenging and would benefit from being paired with a more able student.

Biology • Topic 1 Humans and animals Consolidation

Consolidation

Student's Book page 22
Biology learning objectives
- Know that humans (and some animals) have bony skeletons inside their bodies.
- Know how skeletons grow as humans grow, support and protect the body.
- Know that animals with skeletons have muscles attached to the bones.
- Know how a muscle has to contract (shorten) to make a bone move and muscles act in pairs.
- Explain the role of drugs as medicines.

Resources
- Assessment Sheets B1, B2, B3 and B4

Looking back

Use the summary points to review the key things the students have learned in this topic. Ask questions such as: *Which animals don't have internal skeletons? Which do? In what ways does your skeleton change as you grow? What is a joint? Explain the way muscles help you to move. Can muscles work on their own at joints? Explain why or why not. What is a medicine? What safety precautions should you take with medicines?*

Ask the students to write down three questions of their own about the things they learned in this topic. Let them exchange questions and answer each other's. Get them to check the answers themselves.

How well do you remember?

You may use the revision and consolidation activities on Student's Book page 22 either as a test or as a paired class activity. If you are using the activities as a test, have the students work on their own to complete the tasks in writing and then collect and mark the work. If you are using them as a class activity you may prefer to let the students do the tasks orally. Circulate as they discuss the questions and observe the students carefully to see who is confident and who is unsure of the concepts.

Some suggested answers
1. a bones
   b Answers could include: earthworm, slug, jellyfish.
   c Similarities could include: both have bones; both have a skull, ribs and backbones; both have muscles attached to bones; both have moveable joints.

   Differences could include: elephants do not have arms like we do; their backbone is not upright like ours; they are bigger than humans; their tusks (teeth) stick out in front of their skull while ours are in our mouths; they have a long tail and we do not.
2. It supports the body and allows movement around joints; it protects the internal organs; it grows with you.
3. It can be harmful and potentially life threatening.

Assessment

A more formal assessment of the students' understanding of the topic can be undertaken using Assessment Sheets B1, B2, B3 and B4. These can be completed in class or as a homework task.

Students following Cambridge Primary Science Framework will write progression tests set and supplied by Cambridge International Examinations at this level and feedback will be given regarding their achievement levels.

Assessment Sheet answers

Assessment Sheet B1
1. a, c [2]
2. It supports the body; protects the soft organs inside the body; allows you to stand up and move. [3]
3. a muscles [1]
   b Muscle a (the front thigh muscle or quadriceps) bunches up while muscle b (the back thigh muscle or hamstring) stretches out. [3]
4. When a muscle contracts it pulls against the bone and the bone moves. Muscles cannot push, they can only pull; so they need to work in pairs to allow each joint to move. [2]

Assessment Sheet B2
1. Check students' diagrams. [4]
2. rigid, skeleton, move, supports [4]
3. 206 [1]
4. Answers could include: jellyfish, worm, snail, slug etc. [1]

Assessment Sheet B3
1. tendons, strongest, eye, tired [4]
2. true, true [2]
3. Check students' diagrams. [4]

Assessment Sheet B4
1. a true, b true, c true [3]
2. Drugs that are used to treat illness are called medicines. [1] A drug is any substance that affects how your body works. [1] Medicines can be dangerous if they are not used correctly. [1]
3. prescription, pharmacy [2]
4. ill, immune [2]

Biology • Topic 1 Humans and animals Student's Book answers

Student's Book answers

pages 2–3
1. Other examples include earthworms, caterpillars, octopi, slugs, leeches, sea anemones and so on.
2. Students' own ideas, but the correct answer is no, these animals have an exoskeleton but no bones.
3. Students' should say it feels hard, or that they can feel their bones.
4. It has bones inside it and they maintain its shape.
5. It should indicate to students that we have an internal skeleton with hard bones.

pages 4–5
1. Students' own answers; most should know some bones.
2. Examples of joints are elbow, knee, hip, shoulder, fingers, wrist and so on. Students should also say that each joint allows a person to move.

pages 6–7
1. Students should see that the bones get denser as the person ages; they should also notice an increase in the size of the bones and stronger joints.
2. Their hands would look more like the second picture than the third.
3. Not much happens as growth stops and they do not change again until joints begin to degenerate with age.
4. Cartilage is softer and more flexible than bone.

pages 8–9
1. Students should do the actions.
2. Students' opinions, however the cartilage separates the vertebrae and stops the bones from rubbing together. It also acts like a cushion to protect the bones and absorb shocks.

pages 10–11
1. To make sure they are strong and to form a 'helmet' of immovable and inflexible bone to protect the brain.
2. Their skull contains spaces between the bones, so their brains are vulnerable to knocks and bumps.
3. So that you can chew.
4. The ribs expand and push outwards and then contract and suck inwards as our lungs take in and expel air. The ribs need to be flexible so that we can breathe in and out.

pages 12–13
1. Encourage students to note that the muscles are long and striped; they are, in essence, strong elastic fibre-like structures.
2. So that we can move. They are attached to our bones and they work to move joints, but we also need muscles to survive – our gut, heart and tongue are all examples of muscles.

pages 14–15
1. our bones

pages 16–17
1. Models are simple representations of laws, processes or objects. Models make it easy for us to observe how things work in a simple way so that we can generalise and develop a picture of how the process works in real life.
2. The upper and lower bones of the arm.
3. To make a moveable joint.
4. muscles
5. The fasteners to which the elastics are attached.

pages 18–19
1. Students' own answers.
2. Answers will vary, but students should realise that taking medicines can make them sick and that some medicines could kill them (particularly if they have allergies).

pages 20–21
1. Students' own answers. Examples may include senna, foxglove or a local plant used in traditional medicine.
2. Accept any reasonable answer. A vaccine prevents you from getting a particular disease. Immune means that you are protected from that particular disease and will not contract it.
3. They are harmful and addictive and many people abuse them, so they are strictly controlled.

Biology • Topic 2 Living things in their environment

2.1 The importance of the environment

Student's Book pages 23–25

Biology learning objective
- Investigate how different animals are found in different habitats and are suited to the environment in which they are found.

Resources
- Workbook page 14
- Slideshow B5: Animal habitats
- Slideshow B6: Small animals
- Slideshow B7: Habitats
- Video B1: Flamingos
- Video B2: A coral reef

Classroom equipment
- large sheets of paper
- drawing or colouring equipment

Scientific enquiry skills
- *Obtain and present evidence:* Make relevant observations and comparisons in a variety of contexts; present results in drawings, bar charts and tables.

Key words
- environment
- habitat
- adapted

Scientific background

In Biology we use the term environment to talk about the living (biotic) and non-living (abiotic) components of our surroundings. An environment can refer to the natural features of an area, in which case we talk about the natural environment. However, the environments in which the students find themselves will also contain built elements such as buildings, roads and infrastructure. The school is an environment, as is the home and the larger area in which we live. Living things (plants and animals, at this level) are found in all environments. The place where a plant or animal lives is called its habitat (home). An environment can contain a range of different habitats. For example, you may find spiders and geckoes living in the buildings around you, birds nesting in trees, worms and insects living on plants or in soil, and chickens and goats near homesteads. Living things have specific needs and they are generally found in environments (and particular habitats) where these needs can be met.

In the introduction you will consider flamingos. Flamingos are birds highly suited to their habitats. They have very long legs, webbed feet and oiled feathers, all of which help them to survive in their shallow aquatic habitat. Their beaks are long, pointed and backward-curving for filtering algae and prawns from the shallow water. They can survive in very salty water, such as the shallow salt flats of the Middle East. Those in Lake Nakuru in Kenya are further adapted to live in extremely caustic conditions, but are vulnerable to pollution and drought.

Introduction

- Use the photograph on page 23 of the Student's Book to introduce the idea of flamingos. Explain that flamingos are birds that are well suited to living in salt flats and lakes. Show the class Video B1: Flamingos and discuss how the birds feed and where they live. Explain that flamingos are suited to shallow waters because they have long legs with webbed feet as well as long necks with specially shaped beaks that allow them to feed while their heads are upside down.

- Remind the students that the environment is the scientific name for their surroundings and that the places in which different plants and animals live are called habitats. Ask the students what animals are found in their environment. Let them describe the habitats in which these animals are found.

- Show the class Slideshow B5: Animal habitats. Let the students describe the habitats in which each animal is found. Remind them that animals need their habitat to provide food, water and shelter, and discuss how each habitat provides these.

Biology • Topic 2 Living things in their environment 2.1

Teaching and learning activities

- Turn to Student's Book pages 24 and 25. Let the students work in pairs to describe the habitats shown in each picture and to list the animals found in each. They should list those they can see but also include any that they would expect to find in each place.

- View Video B2: A coral reef with the class. Explain that animals which live in ocean habitats such as these have to be adapted (suited) to life underwater. Let the students name the animals they see and discuss how they are suited to their habitats.

- Show the class Slideshow B6: Small animals. Discuss the habitats in which each animal is likely to be found and how the animal is suited to its habitat. Ask the class whether these animals would be able to survive on a coral reef (no). Let the students explain their answers.

- Return to the Student's Book and let the students work in pairs to complete questions 3 and 4. Share their answers as a class and correct any misconceptions that arise.

Graded activities

1 Students can choose any animal they like (or one of those shown in their books). They may need to do some research to find out about the animal's habitat and how the animal is adapted to suit the conditions found there.

2 Students can either sketch the habitat in normal view or they can draw a plan view (map), which makes it easier to show the elements of the habitat. If they choose to draw a plan view, they should provide a key.

3 Students will need to consider the conditions in the habitat in order to decide which other animals would be well suited to the same conditions.

Consolidate and review

- Show the class Slideshow B7: Habitats. Ask different students to describe the features of each habitat, the conditions they would expect to find in each and which animals would be well suited to such habitats.

- Use Workbook page 14 to consolidate the work done in this lesson. Check the answers to the given task and let the students share their own additions to the table with the class.

Differentiation

■ All of the students should be able to choose an animal and say where it lives. They will be able to name at least one way in which the animal is suited to its habitat. More able students will be able to describe specific physical and/or behavioural adaptations.

● Most of the students should be able to draw a simple sketch of the habitat and label the elements that provide food, shelter and water. More able students will map the habitat and provide detailed answers.

▲ Some of the students should be able to suggest at least two other animals that are suited to the habitat. They will provide detailed lists including a range of types of small invertebrates and different birds (found in most environments).

Big Cat

Any students who have read *Big Cat Africa's big three* may recall some of the other animals that share their habitat with the elephants, rhinos and hippos.

Students who have read *Big Cat The journey of humpback whales* may have insight into how these animals depend on the ocean as their habitat.

Biology • Topic 2 Living things in their environment 2.2

2.2 Adapting to different habitats

Student's Book pages 26–27
Biology learning objectives
- Investigate how different animals are found in different habitats and are suited to the environment in which they are found.

Resources
- Workbook pages 15 to 18
- PCM B4: Polar bear coats
- Slideshow B8: Animal habitats
- Slideshow B9: Jungle habitats
- Slideshow B10: Camels
- Video B3: Animals in their natural habitats
- Video B4: Polar bears

Classroom equipment
- for each group: three lidded containers of cotton wool soaked in warm water; one large container of ice-cold water; a selection of fabrics to represent animal coats, e.g fleece, wool, leather, cotton wool, cotton or linen; one thermometer
- drawing and colouring equipment

Scientific enquiry skills
- *Plan investigative work:* Suggest questions that can be tested and make predictions; communicate these; design a fair test and plan how to collect sufficient evidence; choose apparatus and decide what to measure.
- *Obtain and present evidence:* make relevant observations and comparisons in a variety of contexts; measure temperature, time, force and length.
- *Consider evidence and approach:* Explain what the evidence shows and whether it supports predictions. Communicate this clearly to others.

Key words
- **suited**
- **habitat**
- **adaptation**

⚠️ Students should be careful when working with hot water.

Scientific background

Each environment has its own unique plant and animal life. The plants and animals in an environment interact with each other and depend on the conditions found in the environment for their life processes. At this level, students need to understand that the environment itself influences which plants and animals are found there, and that the plants and animals in an environment are there because they are suited, or adapted, to the conditions found there.

Some animals can only survive in specific conditions. Sharks and whales, for example, can only survive in saltwater environments. Fish need water, but some require fresh water while others need salt water.

A suitable environment is essential for the survival of animals (and plants). Ideally, the environment will supply the animals (and plants) with food, clean water, air, and shelter from the weather and predators. When the environment does not, or cannot, provide what a plant or animal needs, it is unsuitable for that organism.

In this unit you will consider giraffes and polar bears. At 5–6 m tall the giraffe is the tallest living terrestrial mammal. Giraffes have distinctive coat patterns, an extremely long neck and long legs. They are herbivores and mainly eat acacia leaves, which grow high in the trees. Lions can attack giraffes; leopards, spotted hyenas and wild dogs can attack giraffe calves, so it is important that they can spot predators. All giraffes come from Africa, where they live in grasslands and sparsely wooded plains.

Polar bears are found only in the Arctic. They are very well adapted to the harsh conditions in which they live. They have very thick fur with an insulating undercoat, and guard hairs that reflect visible light and make them appear white. Their paws measure up to 30 cm across and help distribute weight when they walk on thin ice. The paws also act as large paddles when the polar bear swims. Polar bears have thick, curved claws that are sharp and strong, which enable them to hold on to the ice and also their prey (seals and large fish).

Biology • Topic 2 Living things in their environment 2.2

Introduction

- Show the class Slideshow B8: Animal habitats. Give students a chance to describe the habitat and to say how the animals shown are well suited to those habitats. Point out that these are artificially created habitats (zoos) but that they have been designed to provide for the animals' needs.

- Explain to the class that you are going to look at some different animals and their habitats in order to find out what features make each animal well suited to its habitat. Tell the class to close their eyes and picture a giraffe. Ask: *What features does a giraffe have that make it different from other animals? Why do you think it has these features?* Then show the class Video B3: Animals in natural habitats, focusing on the giraffe and how it behaves.

Teaching and learning activities

- Turn to page 26 of the Student's Book. Look at the giraffes in the pictures and recap their features. Discuss questions 1 and 2 with the class. Let the students complete Workbook page 15 to summarise their learning.

- Next, tell the class that some animals live in trees. Ask: *Could a giraffe live in a tree? Why not? What do animals that live in trees need?* Show the class Slideshow B9: Jungle habitats. Focus on the ways tree-dwelling animals are suited to climbing and getting food in trees. Use the photographs of monkeys in the Student's Book to talk about the ways in which monkeys are well suited to tree living.

- Students should already know a little about polar bears from earlier stages. Show the class Video B4: Polar bears and talk about where these bears live and what they are like. Focus on the fur of the bear and ask the students to describe its colour and thickness and to say what purpose it serves in this kind of habitat.

Graded activities

1 Refer students back to Video B4: Polar bears and to the photographs on page 27 of the Student's Book as they describe polar bear fur and its purpose.

2 Explain that each group will have three containers containing cotton wool soaked in warm water (to represent a polar bear), a large container with some icy water, a choice of 'coats' for their polar bear and a thermometer. Give the students time to discuss how they are going to carry out their investigation. Take feedback before handing out a copy of PCM B4, which explains how to set up the experiment, to each group. Elicit that taking the temperature of each pot every 5 minutes might be suitable. Students should take readings at least three times and record them in their Workbooks on pages 15–18.

3 As a result of international interest in climate change, students will find it very easy to do this research. There are many articles and programmes about this on the internet.

Consolidate and review

- Spend some time discussing the results of the investigation. Ask one group: *Can you say which you found was the best coat for the bear?* Ask if other groups found the same. If groups had different results, ask: *Why do you think some of the results were different?*

- Use Slideshow B10: Camels to compare the habitat of a camel with those of the other animals studied in this lesson. Focus on the differences and how the camel is well suited to a dry desert habitat.

Differentiation

■ All of the students should be able to describe the fur and its purpose. They will be able to explain that the bears would freeze to death without their fur and also that without it they would have no camouflage.

● Most of the students should be able to record their results and draw their conclusions, although some will need support. They will include notes about their method. More able students should be able to explain how they carried out a fair test and say whether their predictions were correct.

▲ Some of the students should be able to present some findings. They will link polar bear survival to human activity and climate change.

Biology • Topic 2 Living things in their environment 2.3

2.3 Investigating different habitats

Student's Book pages 28–29

Biology learning objective
- Investigate how different animals are found in different habitats and are suited to the environment in which they are found.

Resources
- Workbook pages 19 to 21
- Slideshow B11: Antarctic animals
- Slideshow B12: Desert plants and animals
- Slideshow B13: Animal habitats

Classroom equipment
- map of area around school, if possible
- pens and pencils

Scientific enquiry skills
- *Ideas and evidence:* Collect evidence in a variety of contexts.
- *Plan investigative work:* Choose apparatus and decide what to measure.
- *Obtain and present evidence:* Make relevant observations and comparisons in a variety of contexts; present results in drawing, bar charts and tables.
- *Consider evidence and approach:* Identify simple trends and patterns in results and suggest explanations for some of these.

Key words
- investigate
- habitat

⚠ Students should work in groups or pairs, and clear safety guidelines must be discussed before they do their investigations. Remind them not to touch or harm living organisms.

Scientific background

Observing a habitat and recording what is found there is a fundamental skill in Biology. Scientists do more than simply glance around when they observe organisms in their habitats – they also record what they find, where they find it, and measure (count) how many of each organism they find. The small area that the students are going to investigate is a sample of the larger school environment. Based on what is observed in a sample area, scientists can extrapolate and make decisions about what they would expect to find in the area as a whole.

Introduction

- Revise the concept of a habitat. Ask the students what they understand by the term 'habitat'. Write their ideas on the board (e.g. it's where an animal lives, it has plants in it, it can be destroyed). Explain that there are many different kinds of habitat, some of which they might only have seen on television, e.g. rainforest, desert. Point out that there are many different kinds of habitat around the school, such as flower borders, the school field and playground. Ask the students to make a list of all the habitats they can think of.

- Show the class Slideshow B11: Antarctic animals and use the slides to recap how certain animals are suited to cold environments (there are no polar bears in the slides as these are only found in the Arctic). Ask the class whether these animals would be able to survive in any of the habitats around the school. Make sure they give reasons for their answers.

- Repeat this exercise with Slideshow B12: Desert plants and animals, asking different students to describe the environment and to say how each animal is suited to it.

- Tell the class that they are going to investigate habitats around the school. Ask them to suggest some possible areas for investigation. If you have a map of the area, look at it and discuss where you might find animal habitats.

Biology • Topic 2 Living things in their environment 2.3

Teaching and learning activities

- Turn to Student's Book page 28 and talk about the map. Students should know how to make sense of simple maps. Let them name the environments that have been circled and say what they would expect to find in each (conditions and animals). Once you have discussed this, let the students work in pairs to complete questions 1 and 2. Have a class discussion about their results and try to resolve any disagreements in terms of what would be found in each habitat.
- Remind the class that animals which live in or near water are especially suited to their habitats. Identify the watery habitats on the map. If groups have chosen the pond or the rock pool habitats, let them recap what they would expect in each.
- Let students complete Workbook page 19. This exercise models how to tally, tabulate and graph results and is a useful task to do before the students do their own investigations. Explain how to read tallies if necessary (although students should know how to use these from mathematics lessons). Check their completed graphs to make sure they can draw and label a bar graph.

Graded activities

All students complete all three activities. Differentiation should be provided in the level of support students receive as they work, as well as by outcome (please see guidance in the 'Differentiation' box opposite).

1 Spend some time in the classroom planning the investigation. Students should record their planning on Workbook page 20. Check their plans and discuss the safety aspects of the investigation with the class before allowing the groups to investigate two habitats. Once students have returned to class, they can complete Workbook page 21 to summarise their findings.

2 Encourage the students to choose different animals so they don't all focus on the same one. Before they start, discuss the elements of a fact file using the guidelines on Workbook page 21 so they know what information to include.

3 Allow students to work in pairs or small groups to complete this activity. Allow them to choose any animal they like and let them decide on the format of their presentation. If you have time, let some students present their work to the class.

Consolidate and review

- Talk about the investigations in the class. Compare the two habitats the students investigated and discuss how they were similar and/or different. For different conditions, ask students whether the animals in habitat A would be suited to habitat B. Let them explain why or why not.
- Use Slideshow B13: Animal habitats and let the students develop five questions on the topic. Let them exchange questions and then show the slideshow again, allowing them to answer, and then check, each other's work.
- Play a game in which you display a habitat and then run through a list of different animals, some suited to the habitat and some not. Let the students call out 'suitable' or 'unsuitable' as you name the animals.
- Give students a habitat (one they know or have learned about) and the name of an animal that is not suited to the habitat. Ask them to imagine that they are the animal and to tell their partner why they cannot live in that place.

Differentiation

■ All of the students should be able to answer the questions and give some detail. More able students will consider the questions critically and give reasoned and well-thought-out answers.

● Most of the students should be able to choose an animal and say how it is suited to its habitat. They will be able to complete the fact file with supporting details.

▲ Some of the students will prepare their presentation with little or no help. They should be able to choose an animal that is unsuited to their chosen habitats. Make sure they consider both sets of conditions and choose an animal that suits neither.

Biology • Topic 2 Living things in their environment 2.4

2.4 Identifying and grouping animals

Student's Book pages 30–31

Biology learning objective
- Use simple identification keys.

Resources
- Workbook page 22
- PCM B5: Similarities and differences in birds
- Slideshow B14: Different birds

Classroom equipment
- adverts featuring different types of clothing or electronic products for each group
- paper

Scientific enquiry skills
- *Obtain and present evidence:* Make relevant observations and comparison is a variety of contexts.

Key words
- classification   • key

Scientific background

There is an enormous range of different organisms. Scientists need to name organisms in order to describe their form and function. The name needs to be agreed so that everyone can be sure they are talking about the same organism. The current scientific method of naming organisms (by genus and species) was originated by the Swedish botanist, Carl Linnaeus, who used it for plants. No system is perfect, however; there are always some organisms that do not fit.

Scientists use keys to identify organisms. Keys are often devised using a yes/no system, rather like a flow chart. It is difficult for students to appreciate the value of keys if the organisms they are studying are very different; a key is useful for distinguishing between lions, tigers and leopards, but not between tigers and buffalo. In this unit, the students will be introduced to straightforward keys, but in later stages finer discriminations will be made.

Introduction

- Play a quick game of 'Twenty Questions' in which you think of a member of the class and the students have to work out which one by asking questions to which the answer is 'yes' or 'no'. Make a rule that they are not allowed to use a child's name until they know who it is. Explain that the answers give them a clue that allows them to eliminate some children until they know who it is. For example, if the students ask: *Is it a boy?* and the answer is yes, they can eliminate all the girls. If the answer is no, they can eliminate all the boys. Similarly, questions such as: *Does the student wear glasses? Does the student have long hair?* and so on, will narrow down the field.

- Explain to the class that we place things in groups to make it easier to refer to them. Use the example of a supermarket or clothing store to make the point. When you go into the store, all the spices are in the same place, all the meat is kept together and all the sweets are in the same aisle. Similarly, when you go to buy clothes, the sports clothing is in one place, the footwear is kept together and the sleepwear is in another place. Most stores have boards or signs that act as a key to tell you where to look for different items. Students may have seen these in supermarket aisles, or on boards next to escalators or lifts in shopping malls.

- Give each group some of the adverts you have brought to class. Ask them to sort the items into two groups. Ask: *What yes/no question can you ask to decide whether an item belongs in this group? For example, 'Is it a computer?'* (yes/no) Next, let them divide these groups into two smaller groups. Again, they should articulate a question used to sort the items. For example, *Does it have a keyboard?* If there is enough variety, ask them to split these groups into a further two groups each.

- Draw a flow diagram/decision tree on the board based on one group's sorting. Write the question and draw yes/no arrows from each (refer to the key on page 31 of the Student's Book to see how this is done). Let the students use the key you have drawn up to sort their own items.

Biology • Topic 2 Living things in their environment 2.4

Teaching and learning activities

- Turn to Student's Book pages 30 and 31. Read through the information with the class and discuss what the insects have in common. Then talk about what visible differences the students can see. Explain that scientists place insects in groups by looking at the differences between them. Work through the key with the class to show them how to follow the decision paths.
- Hand out PCM B5: Similarities and differences in birds to the groups. Let them discuss the similarities and differences between the birds then talk about how these could be used to classify the birds and place them in smaller groups. Let the students suggest questions they could ask to sort the birds.
- Show the class Slideshow B14: Different birds. For each bird, let the students suggest a question that could help them to identify that particular bird.

Graded activities

1 Let the students work in pairs to complete this activity. They can use the key on page 31 of the Student's Book, but their instructions should be general and apply to all keys.

2 Let the students work on their own initially. Once they have a rough key, let them pair up with another student to check and discuss their ideas. Let some of the pairs present their keys to the class.

3 Let the students do this activity on their own. Once they have drawn up their keys, let them exchange keys and use them to identify the students involved.

Consolidate and review

- Use Workbook page 22 to consolidate work done on keys. Point out that the birds are all owls and that even a smaller group such as this can be split up using a key to identify the owls.
- Ask the students to explain in their own words what a key is and how it works. Give a few students a chance to share their ideas with the class.

Differentiation

■ Less able students may struggle to organise their thoughts clearly and to write clear instructions. Encourage them to think about what to do first when they see a key, what to do next, and so on. Then ask them to repeat back to you what they did to read the key.

● Most of the students should be able to do this task, although some may struggle with the idea that the first question should relate to whether the bear is living or not living. Some suggested paths are: Is it alive? (no identifies teddy bear); Is it white? (yes identifies polar bear); Is it black and white? (yes identifies panda, no identifies brown bear).

▲ More able students who are thinking critically about this task will choose a range of clearly distinguishable classmates (boys/girls; wearing glasses/not wearing glasses; wearing braces/not wearing braces; long and short hair, and so on).

Biology • Topic 2 Living things in their environment 2.5

2.5 Using identification keys

Student's Book pages 32–33

Biology learning objective
- Use simple identification keys.

Resources
- Workbook page 23
- PCM B6: Small animal card sort
- Slideshow B15: Different fish
- DVD Activity B2: Using an identification key

Classroom equipment
- pictures or cards with names of animals found locally
- reference books
- paper and drawing equipment

Scientific enquiry skills
- *Obtain and present evidence:* Make relevant observations and comparisons in a variety of contexts; present results in drawings, bar charts and tables.

Key word
- **key**

Scientific background

The simple branching keys used here are called dichotomous keys. A dichotomous key is a choice diagram that offers two choices, or paths, based on visible characteristics. The choice you make depends on the organism you are observing. Answering the question will give you a path through the diagram, moving along the branches until you can identify the organism. In reality, scientists would not use keys this simple as the animals shown at this level are all easy to identify.

Introduction

- Give each group one of the small animals from PCM B6. Tell them that this is an unknown animal and that their job is to try to identify it as accurately as possible. Allow the students to use reference books or the computer to try to find out what it is. You are not asking them to identify the exact species, just to be able to identify broadly what type of animal it is. (Answers: beetle, worm, spider, caterpillar, mantis, cicada, stick insect, butterfly.) Then, when the students think that they have identified their organism, ask them how they did so. Focus on what questions they asked to narrow down their choices in each case.

- Explain to the students that they will be trying to group some organisms together according to the features they can see that the organisms have in common. Split the students into small groups and give each group a collection of pictures/photographs/name cards of organisms they might find in the local environment. Ask the students to look carefully at the organisms and try to identify the animals that are similar. When they have identified the similar animals, ask them to record their decisions and give an explanation as to why they have decided they are similar.

Teaching and learning activities

- Turn to the key on Student's Book pages 32 and 33. Look at the pictures of the animals and have a class discussion about similarities and differences. Discuss what characteristics can be used to narrow choices and identify the animals. Work through the key with the class and decide where animals should go.

- Let the students work in pairs, using the key, to answer question 2 and find the most obvious differences between the animals listed.

- Show the class Slideshow B15: Different fish. Again, discuss what all the fish have in common (fins, scales, tail and so on). Then discuss how you can identify different types of fish.

Biology • Topic 2 Living things in their environment 2.5

Graded activities

All students complete all three activities. Differentiation should be provided in the level of support students receive as they work, as well as by outcome (please see guidance in the 'Differentiation' box opposite).

1 Let the students complete this activity on their own. Check their work to make sure they can read, follow and use a key to correctly identify familiar animals. Once they have done this, let them use their completed keys to answer the questions on Workbook page 23. Check the answers orally as a class.

2 Let the students work on their own to do this. They should draw their keys on loose sheets to make it easy to exchange them. Spend some time in class examining and discussing keys that were easy/not so easy to follow.

3 Students need to consider that living things are plants and animals in order to do this task. They can work in pairs to develop a new key. Allow them to share their ideas and solutions with other groups.

Consolidate and review

- Ask the students to prepare a short talk on what keys are used for and why they are so useful in science. They can use examples if they wish.
- Let the students complete an identification key using DVD Activity B2. They can use page 32 of the Student's Book to help them.
- If you have time, the students can use the pictures/names of local animals to develop a key for identifying members of groups.
- Let the students work in groups to draw five different 'alien' beings. Once they have done this, they should decide a name for each one and write it next to the alien. Each group should swap their aliens with another group, with each group working to develop a key to identify the other group's aliens. Once they have finished, each group should give its key to the group that created the aliens, who will check that it works.

Differentiation

■ All of the students need to be able to use the key to identify these animals. They will be able to refer back to the key to answer the questions related to differences between the different animals listed. Assist any students who cannot complete the key.

● Most of the students will be able to develop a different key even if they only rearrange the choices on the given one. More able students will develop a completely new set of choices to sort the animals in different ways.

▲ Some of the students should recognise that this requires adding a choice upfront between plants and animals. Remind them that we start with big groups and then narrow them down.

Biology • Topic 2 Living things in their environment 2.6

2.6 Human activity and the environment

Student's Book pages 34–35

Biology learning objective
- Recognise ways that human activity affects the environment, e.g. river pollution, recycling waste

Resources
- Workbook page 24
- Slideshow B16: Hawksbill turtles
- Slideshow B17: Oil spills
- Slideshow B18: Water pollution

Classroom equipment
- sheets of paper
- coloured pens

Scientific enquiry skills
- *Ideas and evidence:* Collect evidence in a variety of contexts.
- *Obtain and present evidence:* Make relevant observations and comparisons in a variety of contexts.

Key words
- recycling
- pollution

Scientific background

Pollution is anything that harms the environment. Most pollution is a result of human activity. Pollution can change an environment to such an extent that the plants and animals (including humans) in that environment can no longer survive.

Pollution affects the air, the water and the land. Industrial pollution spreads chemicals and waste matter in the air and water. Littering spreads paper, glass and plastic waste over large areas of land. Emissions from vehicles spread toxic substances into the air. Many pathogens (disease-causing organisms) live, and are spread, in polluted water. It is important for students to realise that even water that looks clean can be dangerous to drink.

Water pollution is a major problem. Oceans are polluted by oil spills from ships, by chemicals from industry, by sewage from homes, and by rubbish that is dumped at sea or in the oceans. Water pollution affects how wildlife can survive in the seas and whether we can eat the fish we catch there. Polluted water leads to a decrease in the productivity of the fishing industry, which in turn affects the local economy, as more food may need to be imported from other areas. We can all help to reduce water pollution by measures such as throwing away rubbish properly, using less water, not putting chemicals down the sink and using less fertiliser and pesticide.

Introduction

- Ask the students to think about human activity and how it affects the environment (in both good and bad ways). Let the students work in small groups to draw a concept map about human activity and its positive and negative effects on the environment. They should think back to what they learned in previous stages about the environment and conservation. Circulate as the students work on this task and ask guiding questions if they appear to get stuck.

- Look around your own environment. Identify ways in which people have improved the environment (perhaps by building anti-erosion walls, setting up compost heaps or replanting natural vegetation and/or trees) and ways in which people have damaged the environment (perhaps by building too close to rivers, or by dumping waste or cutting down trees).

- Explain that all human activity has an effect on the environment. Tell the class that you are going to look at some examples to see how this happens, but stress that this is a large topic and that you cannot cover everything involved.

- Show the class Slideshow B16: Hawksbill turtles. Use the opportunity to recap work on animals' suitability for their habitats. Explain that human activity is affecting the turtles' habitats in different ways. Let the students comment and talk about

Biology • Topic 2 Living things in their environment 2.6

the video. Remind them that some human activity impacts positively on the turtles as well, for example in some places beaches are off limits to people and vehicles during the nesting season, and in many places volunteers work hard to rescue baby turtles and make sure they reach the sea safely.

Teaching and learning activities

- Turn to Student's Book pages 34 and 35. Read the information and study the photographs. Answer the questions orally as a class.
- Show Slideshow B17: Oil spills and Slideshow B18: Water pollution. Repeat the Student's Book questions from page 35 in relation to the slides. Ask the students to think of examples of human activity having a more positive effect on water quality.
- Explain that we can think about pollution in terms of cause and effect. Use the water pollution photographs and re-show Slideshow B18, which is about the causes and effects of water pollution. Explain that water pollution is caused by rubbish being dumped in the ocean. This includes chemicals from industries such as desalination, sewage and waste water, and oil from ships. Explain that water pollution can kill wildlife in the ocean; it can contaminate fish so we cannot eat them, and reduces fishing, which in turn means fewer jobs. You will consider cause and effect again in Unit 2.7.

Graded activities

1 Encourage the students to use the photographs as a starting point to find visible clues and evidence of how the environment is being affected by human activity, but also allow them to expand their thinking to consider invisible effects.

2 Students can work in pairs to discuss the sentences and the order in which they should go to form a cohesive paragraph. Once they have produced a paragraph, instruct them to answer the question about their own community on Workbook page 24.

3 It might be useful to structure this discussion as a debate in which some groups argue for one point of view and the other groups take the opposing view. Encourage all students to offer evidence and examples to support their points of view.

Consolidate and review

- In order to reduce the negative effects of human activity, people need to understand that their actions (the causes) have effects and that by changing how we behave, we can make a difference.

  Let the students work in groups to prepare a talk for a) households or b) businesses or c) factory owners to inform them about the effects of their activities and to suggest how they could reduce the negative effects.

- Ask the students, in pairs, to produce an information sheet to inform people how they can reduce the amount of water pollution. They may draw pictures, if they wish, but they must also include text.

Differentiation

■ All of the students should be able to list several effects and also identify effects that cannot be observed on the photographs.

● Most of the students should be able to order the sentences in a way that make sense. They will be able to relate what they have read to their own environment and provide a clear answer to the question. More able students will do additional research and report back more comprehensively on the impact of industrial waste locally.

▲ Some of the students should be able to express an opinion; however, only a few more able students will be able to produce reasoned arguments with examples and evidence to support their points of view.

Big Cat

Any students who have read *Big Cat Fragile Earth* may see connections between human uses of natural resources and impacts on the environment.

Students who have read *Big Cat The journey of humpback whales* may have insight into how creatures that depend on the ocean as their habitat might be affected by the pollution of the oceans.

Biology • Topic 2 Living things in their environment 2.7

2.7 Waste and recycling

Student's Book pages 36–37

Biology learning objective
- Recognise ways that human activity affects the environment e.g. river pollution, recycling waste.

Resources
- Workbook pages 25 and 26
- Image B2: Reduce, reuse, recycle
- Slideshow B19: Reduce, reuse, recycle
- Slideshow B20: Industrial waste

Scientific enquiry skills
- *Ideas and evidence:* Collect evidence in a variety of contexts.
- *Obtain and present evidence:* Make relevant observations and comparisons in a variety of contexts.

Key word
- waste disposal

> ⚠ If students are doing a survey after school, discuss safety issues that are relevant in your community (for example, don't walk around on your own, don't take photographs of people dropping litter, etc.).

Scientific background

Basic awareness can lead to a reduction in pollution; at a very simple level, students can think about the impact of dropping food wrappers on the ground. It is at this level of personal responsibility and how our own actions can make the environment better (or worse) that the topic is covered here.

Disposal of solid waste is a major problem in the world today. Large landfill sites take up valuable land, and cannot be used for many years after they become full because of the toxic chemicals leaching into the ground, particularly from heavy metals. Solid waste usually decomposes over many years. The decomposition process also produces methane gas, which is explosive. If this is trapped and harnessed, it may be burned and converted to electricity. Many substances will not biodegrade and have to be incinerated. This can release poisonous gases into the atmosphere. Ways to reduce the problems of waste disposal include sorting waste, recycling (metals, plastics, glass, paper) and turning food waste into compost. Waste also attracts wild animals and rats, which carry disease.

Thanks to new technologies and factories, many items can be recycled, including all glass, most plastics, all cans, most metal, rubber, most paper and cardboard, CDs, printer cartridges, fluorescent bulbs and batteries. Some of these materials can be reused in the same form; others can be made into completely new materials, for example, a process has been developed to turn rubber tyres into diesel!

Some objects, such as plastic cups, plastic bottle tops, margarine tubs, plastic film, aluminium foil, crisp packets and plastic cutlery, cannot be recycled.

Introduction

- Ask the students to think about and write down all the things they throw away on a normal day. Read out some of the lists and have a class discussion about what happens to these things.
- Turn to Student's Book page 36 and look at the image of waste. Answer questions 1 to 3 as a class.
- Show Image B2 and Slideshow B19: Reduce, reuse, recycle. Focus on the Reduce, Reuse, Recycle logo. Ask the students what the logo means. Remind the students, if necessary, that recycling helps the world sustain the environment in which we all live by reducing demand upon natural resources, for example by recycling old newspapers to make new paper. Explain that countries all over the world use the logo to encourage people to produce less waste.

Teaching and learning activities

- Ask the students, in pairs, to write a list of reasons why we should reuse or recycle things. Then ask the pairs to combine to form groups of four and

Biology • Topic 2 Living things in their environment 2.7

compare their lists. Take feedback across the class and build up a list on the board. Ensure that groups mention, in addition to the need to conserve resources, that: waste can pollute the environment and can harm wildlife; landfill sites are too full; burning waste pollutes the air; we can save energy (and hence fuels, and again reduce air pollution) by recycling rather than making new.

- Remind the students that water is a valuable resource and that we need to take steps to protect and conserve water sources. Discuss questions 4 and 5 (on Student's Book page 37) as a class.
- Ask students to complete Workbook page 25. Remind them that they thought about cause and effect in the previous lesson.
- Explain that industrial waste often ends up in water supplies. Show the students Slideshow B20, which has images of industrial waste. As they watch the slides, they should make notes in preparation for writing three questions to ask about each image. Describe whether each image shows solid, liquid or gas pollution. Explain that these are all types of pollution, and that liquids can pollute water and gases can pollute the air. Let students work with a partner and use their notes to write three questions. Discuss their questions and try to answer as many as possible. Refer to the 'Scientific background' above. If the students ask any questions you cannot answer, tell them that they (and you) may find out during the lesson. Otherwise, say that you will do some research to find out.

Graded activities

1 Let students compile a personal list first. Then let them work in groups to produce a consolidated list. Share the lists as a class and allow students to add to their lists as they hear new ideas. Check any controversial items by getting the students to do some research to find out whether the item is recyclable or not.

2 Students can either do this as a practical task or they can do a survey using secondary sources and/or interviews with community members.

3 Let the students decide on the format of their presentation. Encourage them to think carefully about what might make people want to recycle and to use this to encourage people to do so (persuasive writing).

Consolidate and review

- Ask the students to make a list of all the different ways of dealing with items that we no longer want or need. Ensure that they know about any recent waste management schemes in your community.
- Let the students work in groups to prepare a 'waste hotspot' map of their local area. These should show where there is a problem with waste as well as where waste can be safely disposed of or recycled. If this is a serious problem in your area you might like to consider letting the students develop an awareness campaign to try to improve the situation.
- Use Workbook page 26 to consolidate learning and to check that the students have understood the work in this unit.

Differentiation

■ All of the students should be able to produce a basic list of about five items. More able students should be able to add at least 10 items, and some students will produce comprehensive and detailed lists.

● Most of the students will think critically and creatively to answer the questions. More able students will produce detailed reports highlighting issues and suggesting improvements.

▲ Some of the students should be able to explain some of the positive effects of recycling. They will produce interesting and entertaining presentations that make their point clearly and which encourage recycling by showing how it can benefit people and the environment.

Biology • Topic 2 Living things in their environment Consolidation

Consolidation

Student's Book page 38

Biology learning objectives

- Investigate how different animals are found in different habitats and are suited to the environment in which they are found.
- Use simple identification keys.
- Recognise ways that human activity affects the environment, e.g. river pollution, recycling waste.

Resources

- PCM B7: Identifying wild cats
- Assessment sheets B5, B6 and B7

Looking back

Use the summary points to review the key things the students have learned in this topic. Ask the students to make a concept map to summarise what they have learned. Encourage them to use the summary points as a basis for developing headings/topics for their concept map.

Write a set of true and false statements related to concepts in this chapter. Hand these out and let the students sort them into two groups. Use the false statements and ask the students to rewrite these to make them true.

How well do you remember?

You may use the revision and consolidation activities on Student's Book page 38 either as a test or as a paired class activity. If you are using the activities as a test, have the students work on their own to complete the tasks in writing and then collect and mark the work. If you are using them as a class activity you may prefer to let the students do the tasks orally. Circulate as the students discuss the questions and observe them carefully to see who is confident and who is unsure of the concepts. If you are doing the tasks orally, you can reach a consensus about which answers are correct.

Some suggested answers

1. a A – seabirds, lizards, crabs, fish, small tree birds, fruit bats; B – worms, ants, beetles, mice; C – giraffes, antelope, lizards, birds of prey, vultures, rodents; D – fish, tadpoles, frogs, crabs, water beetles, snails, slugs.
   b Answers will vary depending on which animals students have listed.
2. a = lion, b = black panther, c = tiger
   d = Does it have a thin body and long legs? Or: Are its spots arranged in groups?
3. Causes: littering, run off, industrial spills, waste from fishing, dumping on land near the river. Effects: water quality is poor, fish die, animals move away, diseases can be spread.

Assessment

A more formal assessment of the students' understanding of the topic can be undertaken using Assessment Sheets B5, B6 and B7. These can be completed in class or as a homework task.

Students following Cambridge Primary Science Framework will write progression tests set and supplied by Cambridge International Examinations at this level and feedback will be given regarding their achievement levels.

Assessment Sheet answers

Assessment Sheet B5

1. Neck: to reach the leaves on tall trees; legs: to reach the leaves on tall trees; coat: to help camouflage them from lions. [3]
2. claws – These are curved to help the polar bear to grip the ice. paws – These are wide and flat to help the polar bear to walk on the snow. fur – This provides camouflage. nose – This is very sensitive to allow the polar bear to find other animals to hunt. [4]
3. It can climb trees using its hands, feet and tail. It eats fruits, nuts and leaves that grow in the forest. [2]
4. Answers might include: fish, frog, toad, water snail, water flea, etc. [1]

Assessment Sheet B6

1. Check students' diagrams. [4]
2. Accept any reasonable answers. For example: a spider has eight legs, caterpillars have more. A slug has no legs, a woodlouse has more; or: a woodlouse has body segments, a slug does not. An owl comes out at night, a duck does not; or: a duck can swim on water, an owl cannot. [3]
3. true, false, true [3]

Assessment Sheet B7

1. Answers might include: the water is unsafe to drink, it can destroy a habitat and kill the plants and animals that live there. [2]
2. false, true [2]
3. rubbish, harmful, waste [3]
4. newspaper, drinks can, glass [3]

Biology • Topic 2 Living things in their environment Student's Book answers

Student's Book answers

pages 24–25
Answers will vary.
1 Environment A contains rock pools, salt water, sand banks, some bushes and steep cliffs. Environment B is forested, with tall trees, bushes and lots of undergrowth; the soil is likely to be damp and dark.
2 Environment A: seagulls (and other sea birds), cormorants, oystercatchers, limpets, crabs, starfish, fish, anemones. Environment B: birds, rabbits, hedgehogs, insects and other small creatures in the soil.
3 Seabirds have webbed feet and sharp beaks for eating shelled animals; starfish and limpets cling to rocks; anemones can close when the tide is out. Rabbits have fur to keep them warm and they can hide in the undergrowth; birds have sharp beaks for eating seeds and fruits; hedgehogs eat worms and slugs in the damp soil; insects feed on flowers and make their homes in the plants and ground.
4 Both rabbits and butterflies need soft edible plants to survive – these don't grow in rock pools. They are also not suited to living in salt water.

pages 26–27
1 It allows it to feed on the tips of trees at a height and to see a long distance to spot predators.
2 The spotty coat helps camouflage them; their tongue acts like a finger (it is prehensile) to pull leaves off trees and allows the giraffe to eat thorns; the ability to withstand dry conditions means the giraffe can survive well in the dry season by eating leaves alone.
3 They are able to climb trees; their tails help them balance; their hands and feet are able to hold onto branches, but also allow them to pick and hold fruit and seeds. Their fur keeps them warm and offers some camouflage.
4 Cold oceans with icebergs.
5 They have long thick white fur to keep them warm and to camouflage them, but black skin to retain heat. They have big paws with sharp claws and strong jaws with sharp teeth to kill and eat seals. They can swim.

pages 28–29
1 Answers will vary depending on what the students choose.
2 Answers will vary depending on what the students choose.

pages 30–31
1 They have six legs and jointed bodies divided into a head, thorax and abdomen.
2 The ant does not have wings; the ladybird has spots; the grasshopper has an external skeleton and strong back legs, and so on.

pages 32–33
1 a – fly larva, b – snail, c – worm, d – aphid, e – spider, f – woodlouse, g – centipede, h – slug, i – millipede
2 Spider has 8 legs, woodlouse has more; snail has a shell, slug does not; centipede has two legs per segment, millipede has more; a worm has many body segments, a fly larva has fewer.

pages 34–35
1 Answers will vary, but students should realise that the activities produce waste products that enter the water around the industries.
2 Waste could be stored in tanks and not released into the water; impurities could be removed before any waste is released into the water; industries could be located elsewhere.
3 It poisons or kills fish. Animals that eat the fish are also affected. In many cases, pollutants allow nutrients to bloom in the water and they use up all the oxygen, so fish suffocate.
4 It is unsightly and unhealthy. Pollution often means water sources cannot be used, drinking water supplies become unsafe, fish are too toxic to eat or they die and there is no food source for people living near the water, and so on.

pages 36–37
1 Students' answers will depend on how waste is disposed of locally.
2 It has to be dumped, causing unsightly landfills, or burned, increasing air pollution.
3 Students' own suggestions, but they should include reduce, reuse and recycle options.
4 plastic
5 It is thrown away on land and blows into the water, or it flows in through storm water drains when it rains, or it is simply thrown into the water by careless people.

Chemistry • Topic 3 States of matter

3.1 States of matter

Student's Book pages 39–41

Chemistry learning objective
- Know that matter can be solid, liquid or gas.

Resources
- Workbook pages 27–28
- Slideshow C1: States of matter
- Slideshow C2: Liquids
- Slideshow C3: Gases in action
- Video C1: Solid, liquid, gas

Classroom equipment
- for the demonstration: block of ice, bowl of water and kettle with boiling water to show steam as a gas
- for each group: samples of five different everyday solids, five different liquids (such as milk, oil, water, juice and honey), balloon full of air, two different containers of different shapes
- plastic sheets for waterproofing
- poster materials

Scientific enquiry skills
- *Ideas and evidence:* Test an idea or prediction based on scientific knowledge and understanding.
- *Plan investigative work:* Suggest questions that can be tested and make predictions; communicate these.
- *Consider evidence and approach:* Identify simple trends and patterns in results and suggest explanations for some of these; link evidence to scientific knowledge and understanding in some contexts.

Key words
- matter
- states
- solid
- liquid
- gas

> ⚠ Warn the students that spillages will make the floor slippery. Make sure all spillages are cleaned up.

Scientific background

Solids, liquids and gases are the three main states of matter. With a few exceptions, nearly all materials can take these three forms.

Solids are characterised by their fixed shape and inability to flow or to be compressed. Many solids, such as flour, sugar, salt, sand and rice, appear to have the ability to flow. When they are poured, they move and take the shape of any container they occupy. However, the individual particles are still solid. A grain of sugar has a fixed shape, cannot flow and does not take the shape of its container. It is only when many grains are put together that they appear to take on the properties of a liquid.

Liquids take the shape of any container, can flow, have a surface and cannot be compressed easily. Liquids also flow to the lowest level they possibly can, under the force of gravity. The measure of an amount of a liquid is called its 'volume'. The volume of a liquid does not change when you transfer it between containers, even if the shape of its container does.

Gases also take the shape of any container and can flow. They can be compressed easily.

Many materials cannot be classified strictly as solids, liquids or gases because they are a mixture. For example, fizzy drinks are gases (carbon dioxide) compressed into liquid (water).

Introduction

- Write the words 'solid', 'liquid' and 'gas' in three separate columns on the board. Tell the students that these are the three main states of matter and nearly all materials take these three forms. Show the students a block of ice, a bowl of water and steam coming from a kettle. Ask: *Which one of these do you think is a solid? Which is a liquid? Which is a gas? Why do you think this?* Ask the students for other examples of solids, liquids and gases. Establish what they think the words solid, liquid and gas mean. Try to establish a class description and list examples for each state of matter. Record these on the board.
- Show the class Slideshow C1: States of matter. Ask the students to identify the different substances and to say whether they are solid, liquid or gas. Check

Chemistry • Topic 3 States of matter 3.1

that each item meets the criteria the students have identified in their class descriptions.

- Show the students Video C1 of materials that are solid, liquid or gas. Ask the students to identify further examples of solids, liquids and gases from the video. Ask: *Do you want to change or add to the class descriptions?*

Teaching and learning activities

- Turn to Student's Book pages 40 and 41. Use the text and photographs to confirm the definitions and to begin to talk about the properties of matter in its different states.
- Use Slideshow C2: Liquids to demonstrate that liquids flow and take the shape of a container. Explain that gases are more difficult to observe as we cannot see them around us in most cases. Use Slideshow C3: Gases in action to introduce different gases and to show the students that gases can be compressed and put into a container (such as the oxygen cylinder) but that they can also spread out and mix with air.
- Look at the photographs on Student's Book page 41. Let the students work in pairs to answer the questions and identify the state of different items in the photograph.
- Explain to the class that they are going to use different materials to explore the properties of matter. Stress that it is the properties of a substance that we use to classify it. So, for example, even though a fizzy drink may contain gas, it behaves more like a liquid and is therefore considered to be liquid.

Graded activities

1 Let the learners work in groups to discuss this and to decide what properties or characteristics they would use to decide whether a substance is solid, liquid or gas. Encourage them to express these in the form of questions (as that is what you would ask about a substance to make your decision).

2 Tell the students that they are going to look at different materials. They need to classify them as solid, liquid or gas by testing some of the properties. Ask the students to: squash the material; see if it flows; see what happens when it is placed in different containers. Use conventional solids, liquids and gases at this stage. Blow air into a balloon to explore the gas. Ask the students to record their findings on page 27 of the Workbook.

3 Encourage the students to watch the slideshows showing liquids and gases again before they draw up their tables.

Consolidate and review

- Spend some time talking about the investigation and what the students learned from their experiences. Select different students to give feedback. Sum up by concluding that: solids have a fixed shape, cannot flow and cannot be squashed; liquids take the shape of any container, can flow and cannot be squashed; gases take the shape of any container, can flow and can be squashed.
- Use Workbook page 28 to consolidate the work in this unit and to make sure the students realise that some matter is a mixture of states.
- Ask the students to draw their own posters about solids, liquids and gases. They should summarise the properties and give a few examples of each state. They can add photographs or pictures cut from magazines to add visual appeal.

Differentiation

■ All of the students should be able to distinguish between the states, although they may struggle to express these differences in scientific language. Assist those students who struggle by asking them questions that model the language. For example, if they say liquids are runny, ask: *So are you saying that a liquid can flow?*

● Most of the students should be able to describe the properties of solids, liquids and gases in terms of their shape, flow and ability to be squashed. More able students should be able to provide less familiar examples and describe differences in properties between different solids and liquids.

▲ Some of the students will need little or no help to complete their tables. They will be able to tell the difference between the two states, but some may struggle to compare the two using correct scientific terms.

Chemistry • Topic 3 States of matter 3.2

3.2 Water

Student's Book pages 42–43
Chemistry learning objective
- Know that matter can be solid, liquid or gas.

Resources
- Workbook page 29
- DVD Activity C1: Water cycle

Classroom equipment
- for the demonstration: block of ice, bowl of water and kettle with boiling water to show steam as a gas
- for each group: large metal or plastic bowl; large bowl; small yogurt pot; plastic cup; plastic film; water; small weight; sunny window sill
- maps, books, magazines, CD-ROMs or access to the internet
- paper
- colouring equipment

Scientific enquiry skills
- *Ideas and evidence:* Collect evidence in a variety of contexts; test an idea or prediction based on scientific knowledge and understanding.

Key words
- water
- gaseous
- vapour
- change of state
- water cycle

⚠️ Warn the students that spillages will make the floor slippery. Make sure all spillages are cleaned up.

Scientific background

The three states of matter are solid, liquid and gas. For the material to change from one state to the next (solid to liquid to gas) heat energy must be applied to the material for melting (solid to liquid) or evaporation (liquid to gas) to take place. At the point of change of state (melting from solid to liquid), the heat energy is needed to pull the particles apart. This also happens at the point of boiling from liquid to gas.

Solid and liquid states can change at specific temperatures, depending on the material in question. They are reversible, through heating or cooling. Water, for example, in its solid form (ice) melts when heated above 0 °C, becoming liquid water, but freezes again to a solid when cooled back to 0 °C.

Water can be a liquid, a gas or a solid and we can see these three states on the Earth's surface and in its atmosphere. Water is constantly being evaporated, condensed, frozen and melted, and this takes place in what we call the water cycle. The heat energy from the Sun evaporates water from lakes, oceans, streams and rivers. This water vapour then rises and, when it reaches cold air in the atmosphere, condenses to form clouds. When clouds are saturated they release water as rain and this continuous cycle starts again.

Introduction

- Show the class the ice, water and steam (from a kettle). Ask them what these three things have in common (they are different states of water). Explain that water is a common type of matter and that we can easily observe it and see how it changes state. Look at the photographs on Student's Book page 42 and discuss the questions orally as a class. Remember that students may not have the technical terms to describe evaporation and/or condensation at this stage, so allow them to say things such as 'the water turns to a gas and goes into the air'.

- Ask the class: *Where does rain come from?* Allow some discussion and then show the students DVD Activity C1, about the water cycle, or use the picture on page 43 of the Student's Book. Explain the water cycle in simple terms, and discuss ideas about where water comes from and how it is used. States of matter such as liquid and gas, and changes of state such as evaporation and condensation, will be covered later in this topic. If the students ask questions beyond the scope of this lesson, explain that they will learn more later in the course.

Chemistry • Topic 3 States of matter 3.2

Teaching and learning activities

- Ask the students, in their groups, to look at page 43 of the Student's Book. Ask them to take turns to describe the process of the water cycle. Tell them to listen carefully and remind each other of any omissions. Go from group to group and ask them to explain the water cycle to you. The students can work together to do this.
- Discuss questions 4 and 5 with the class. Make sure they can identify where water is liquid, solid and gas in the water cycle. Also make sure they understand that a cycle is a repeating process that continues endlessly (a loop).

Graded activities

1 Look again at the DVD activity of the water cycle before doing this activity. Encourage the students to think about what happens to a drop of water as it moves through the cycle. Then let the students discuss and draw their own cartoon stories. Display the comics in the classroom or combine them to make a class booklet.

2 Discuss the process of modelling with the class and read through the instructions on Workbook page 29. Make sure the groups know what they are to do and then let them set up their models. You may need to leave these on the windowsill overnight in order to see results (depending on the temperature where you live). Ask the students to predict what they think will happen.

3 Let the students complete this activity on their own. They can use labelled diagrams to make their points, but they must add some text to the explanations.

Consolidate and review

- Discuss the models and what they show. Stress that this process is similar to the water cycle. Water evaporates from lakes, seas and oceans and then condenses high in the atmosphere, where it is colder, forming clouds. The water droplets join together and eventually get too big to stay in the cloud. The clouds are saturated with water so the water falls back to Earth as rain, hail or snow.
- Tell the students that they are going to make a display poster about the water cycle. Say that they are to work in groups of three or four, and they all need to have jobs – drawing pictures, writing, cutting pictures from magazines or finding information. Have lots of resources available, such as maps, books, magazines, CD-ROMs or the internet. Give the students time to work on their posters in class, but allow them to finish the posters in a later lesson if necessary.

Differentiation

■ All of the students should be able to draw a simple comic story showing at least the processes of rising from the surface as a gas and falling back to Earth as rain. More able students will produce detailed stories with a good understanding of how the water might feel/react as it evaporates, condenses and so on.

● Most of the students should be able to give a basic overview of the water cycle and will know that evaporation and condensation are involved (even if they don't use those terms). More able students should be able to talk about each stage of the water cycle and the processes that take place. They should show a good understanding of the water cycle, use key words and talk confidently about the processes involved at each stage.

▲ Some of the students should be able to explain that the model is a simplification of the natural process. They will produce detailed reports highlighting shortcomings in the model.

Chemistry • Topic 3 States of matter 3.3

3.3 Heating matter

Student's Book pages 44–45
Chemistry learning objectives
- Investigate how materials change when they are heated and cooled.
- Know that melting is when a solid turns into a liquid and is the reverse of freezing.

Resources
- Workbook pages 30–31
- Video C2: Changes of state
- Video C3: Butter melting
- Video C4: Volcanoes
- DVD Activity C2: Heating materials

Classroom equipment
- thermometers
- for each group for Activity 1: ice cubes; tray or bowl
- for each group for Activity 2: bowls for hot water; four small foil dishes; four different substances, e.g. ice, chocolate, metal, cube of jelly

Scientific enquiry skills
- *Plan investigative work:* Design a fair test and plan how to collect sufficient evidence; choose apparatus and decide what to measure.
- *Obtain and present evidence:* Make relevant observations and comparisons in a variety of contexts; measure temperature, time, force and length; present results in drawings, bar charts and tables.
- *Consider evidence and approach:* Explain what the evidence shows and whether it supports predictions. Communicate this clearly to others; link evidence to scientific knowledge and understanding in some contexts.

Key words
- **melted**
- **heating**

> ⚠ Ensure that the water is not hot enough to scald. Warn students about the dangers of hot water and the need for good behaviour. Tell them not to put their hands in hot water or to put anything in their mouths. Mop up any spilled water immediately.

Scientific background

Melting happens when heat energy is added to a substance and the energy pulls the particles apart from each other. This causes the material to change state from a solid to a liquid. When the substance is cooled and loses its heat energy, it becomes a solid again. Different substances melt at different temperatures – they have different melting points. Metals have very high melting points because the forces between the atoms are very strong and a lot of energy is required to overcome them.

Introduction

- Show the class Video C2 of ice melting. Ask the students to note down descriptive words or properties to describe what they see as they watch the video. Ask them to discuss with a partner what they saw happening to the ice. Take feedback from the students, listing their ideas and words on the board. Ask: *Why did the ice melt?*

- Move the discussion on to changes of state. Talk about solid water becoming liquid water through the heat energy being transferred from the surroundings to the ice cube. Show Video C3 of butter melting and discuss why the pan doesn't melt. Ask the students to look at page 44 in the Student's Book. Encourage them to discuss, in pairs, what is happening in the pan. Lead the students to understand that the butter melts more easily than the pan because the pan is made of metal.

- Ask: *Would chocolate or an ice cube melt first, under the same conditions? Why do some materials melt more easily than others?* Students should conclude that different materials need different amounts of heat (energy) to change from solid to liquid.

- Show Video C4 of volcanoes. Explain that metals and rocks melt at very high temperatures (from about 800 °C upwards).

Chemistry • Topic 3 States of matter 3.3

Teaching and learning activities

In this unit, the investigations function as the teaching and learning activities. Before tackling these, make sure the students can use a thermometer to take temperature. Ask a few students to read the temperature at three very different places in the classroom, for example inside a refrigerator or a cool bag, by a windowsill in full sunlight and in the shade, under a table.

Graded activities

1 Set the students the following challenge: *Who can make an ice cube melt the fastest?* Explain that they will all have an ice cube of the same size and they have to choose where in the classroom it will melt most quickly. You can restrict the choices to places such as in the light at the window or in a dark drawer.

Ask the groups to discuss the variables involved for a few minutes. Ask: *What do you need to do to make this a fair test?* Provide a tray or bowl for each ice cube and allow up to 20 minutes for the ice cubes to melt. Students should check their ice cubes every 5 minutes and record their observations on page 30 of the Workbook. After 20 minutes, ask the class to compare observations and discuss results.

2 Tell the students that they are going to investigate melting points of materials. Give each group a bowl containing hot water, four small foil dishes to float on the water, and four different substances, for example ice, chocolate, metal, cube of jelly. Ask the groups how they can make their investigation a fair test. Briefly take feedback and review their ideas. Ask them to make a prediction about which material will melt the fastest and which will melt the slowest. Tell them to put a different sample in each dish. All results should be recorded on page 31 of the Workbook.

3 Students can complete this activity in small groups. The information is easy to find in books or on the internet.

Consolidate and review

- Discuss what happened to the ice cubes in the different areas. Ask: *Which ice cube melted fastest? Which one melted slowest? Why did they melt at different speeds?* Talk about the heat energy melting the ice cubes and the temperatures around the room affecting the rate at which the ice melted. Ask: *Was the experiment a fair test? Was there anything you needed to do differently?*

- Ask the groups to report back with their findings and to explain their results. Ask: *Which material took the longest to melt? Which was the quickest? Can anyone describe what happened when the substance started to melt?* Finally, ask: *Why did some substances take longer to melt than others?* Explain that some substances need more heat energy and therefore need to be hotter to be able to melt. The hot water they used was at less than 100 °C. Some substances (like metals) need temperatures of thousands of degrees to melt.

- Let students complete DVD Activity C2 as reinforcement and consolidation.

- Ask students to think of examples where it is useful for materials to melt at different temperatures. What would happen if, for example, an ice-cream cone melted before the ice cream? Tell them to think of another example, describe which material melts first and why this is so.

Differentiation

■ All of the students should be able to state that the ice cube stored at the highest temperature will melt first. They should be able to explain why temperature is not the only thing that affects how quickly a solid melts; the amount of solid is also important.

● Most of the students should be able to name different materials that melt at different temperatures. They should be able to explain why materials melt at different temperatures.

▲ Some of the students should be able to provide detailed and technical information, including references to melting points.

Chemistry • Topic 3 States of matter 3.4

3.4 Cooling matter

Student's Book pages 46–47

Chemistry learning objectives

- Investigate how materials change when they are heated and cooled.
- Know that melting is when a solid turns into a liquid and is the reverse of freezing.

Resources

- Workbook pages 32–33
- Slideshow C4: Different shaped solids
- Video C2: Changes of state
- DVD Activity C3: Solids and liquids

Classroom equipment

- thermometers
- for the demonstrations: ice cube; piece of chocolate; small metal block; candle wax grated into clear bowl; large bowl of hot water; mould to pour molten wax into
- for each group: molten samples of chocolate, butter and water; small foil dishes for each; foil plate; large bowl of crushed ice; timer

Scientific enquiry skills

- *Obtain and present evidence:* Make relevant observations and comparisons in a variety of contexts; measure temperature, time, force and length; present results in drawings, bar charts and tables.
- *Consider evidence and approach:* Explain what the evidence shows and whether it supports predictions. Communicate this clearly to others; link evidence to scientific knowledge and understanding in some contexts.

Key words
- **freezing**
- **cooling**

⚠️ Ask the students to collect the molten liquid samples in a small metal foil dish on a foil plate so they do not have to touch them. The students need to take care with their thermometers.

Scientific background

When a liquid cools to become a solid, it solidifies. Water solidifies at 0 °C, but other materials solidify at much higher temperatures. Chocolate, for example, solidifies at room temperature. In science, freezing means the same as solidifying, so freezing is not just a term used for water turning to ice. This can cause confusion.

Changes of state such as melting, freezing, evaporating and condensing are reversible. In all of these examples the material can be 'got back' to its original state or shape using the reverse process (melting/freezing and evaporation/condensation). Examples of these changes include ice melting into water and solid chocolate melting into a liquid.

Introduction

- Show the students an ice cube, a piece of chocolate that has been formed into a shape and some metal that has been moulded. Ask: *In what way have these materials been shaped?* Establish that they had to be melted, put into a mould and cooled until they became hard. Show the class Slideshow C4: Different shaped solids to provide them with different examples.
- Demonstrate melting and freezing with wax. Place some grated candle wax in a clear bowl, in a bowl of hot water. The students can observe it melting. Now pour it into a small mould. After a minute or two, show the students that the candle wax is no longer a liquid, it has become a solid. Ask them to discuss this in pairs and work out how it has happened. The students should conclude that the liquid has cooled when taken away from the heat and turned back into a solid. Introduce the term 'freezing' by writing it on the board and asking the students to repeat it. Also reintroduce the term 'reversible', which means able to change back. Establish that melting and freezing are reversible.

Chemistry • Topic 3 States of matter 3.4

Teaching and learning activities

- Turn to Student's Book page 46 and 47. Use the photographs to talk about cooling and freezing and answer the questions orally with the class.
- Use Video C2: Changes of state to review what happens to materials when they are heated and cooled. Let the students make notes and then describe what they saw on the video using the correct scientific terms.
- Remind the students that we use a thermometer to measure temperature. Let a few students take turns to explain how to use a thermometer safely and correctly.

Graded activities

1 Let the students work independently to complete this task. If drawing a thermometer is too difficult, you may want to provide them with a blank template to use instead.

2 Tell the students that you are going to give them molten samples of materials. Ask them to think about how to carry out an investigation to test which sample freezes first. Ask: *In what ways will you make the test fair?* Take responses from the groups and agree on a method to make the test fair. Establish that groups will each need the same amount of molten liquid (half-fill a small foil dish) starting at the same temperature, a cool container (a bowl full of ice) to put the materials in, and a timer to see which material freezes first. They will need to record when freezing starts and take the temperature at that time. Have molten chocolate, butter and water ready in hot water baths. Ask the students to carry out the investigation. Put the liquids into the small metal dishes when the students are ready to collect them and place these on a foil plate for carrying. The students can record their predictions and results on page 32 of their Workbook.

3 Students can work in pairs to do the research and discuss what they find out.

Consolidate and review

- Write the words 'solid' and 'liquid' on the board and discuss what the students already know about these two words. Explain that solid and liquid are states of matter, that solids can turn to liquids and liquids can turn into solids through the changes of state (melting or freezing) and that these changes are reversible. Draw arrows on the board to show how states of matter can change from one to the other and back. Let the class complete DVD Activity C3.
- Use Workbook page 33 to consolidate learning and assess students' understanding of the melting/solidifying processes.

Differentiation

■ All of the students should be able to read a thermometer. Some of them may struggle to write clear instructions. Assist these students by producing a set of instructions for them to order or a writing frame that provides a structure for this.

● Most of the students should be able to talk about liquids getting cold and going solid. They should be able to give examples of liquids solidifying at different temperatures, for example wax, butter, water, chocolate. More able students should be able to discuss energy changes during freezing and/or changes to the particles.

▲ Some of the students should be able to find definitions of the terms and will be able to rephrase these in their own words. They will be able to clearly explain why the melting and freezing point are in fact the same, as this is where the 'change of state' takes place in both directions.

Big Cat

Students who have read *Big Cat Antarctica: Land of the penguins* will know that this part of the world is covered by ice – water in its solid state.

Chemistry • Topic 3 States of matter 3.5

3.5 Liquid to gas

Student's Book pages 48–49
Chemistry learning objectives
- Investigate how materials change when they are heated and cooled
- Observe how water turns into steam when it is heated but on cooling the steam turns back into water.

Resources
- Workbook page 34
- Video C5: Boiling and steam
- DVD Activity C4: Key words

Classroom equipment
- for each group: three open containers of different diameters; measuring cylinder; water

Scientific enquiry skills
- *Ideas and evidence:* Test an idea of prediction based on scientific knowledge and understanding.

- *Plan investigative work:* Suggest questions that can be tested and make predictions; communicate these; Design a fair test and plan how to collect sufficient evidence; choose apparatus and decide what to measure.
- *Consider evidence and approach:* Identify simple trends and patterns in results and suggest explanations for some of these; explain what the evidence shows and whether it supports predictions. Communicate this clearly to others.

Key words
- evaporate
- steam

⚠ Keep the students well away from the heat source and boiling water.
Warn the students that spillages will make the floor slippery. Make sure all spillages are cleaned up promptly.

Scientific background

Evaporation is a change of state. It causes a liquid to change to a gas. This can happen when liquids are cold or hot. Evaporation is greater when the temperature is higher because the liquid particles or molecules have more energy and move faster, so the likelihood that a particle will escape or evaporate from the liquid is greater. Evaporation only occurs at the surface of a liquid, where the liquid molecules are able to escape into the air and become a gas, so the bigger the surface area the greater the evaporation. Movement of air over the surface of a liquid will also increase the rate of evaporation. Boiling differs from evaporation because the whole liquid is changing state at a specific temperature.

A high rate of evaporation will help things dry quickly: a low rate will cause things to dry slowly. If there is a large surface area, with lots of air movement, and the temperature is high, then evaporation will happen quickly. If the temperature is low, the air is still and the surface area is small, then the rate of evaporation will be slow.

Introduction

- Spray some perfume into a shallow dish. It will quickly disappear. Ask: *Where did it go? What state of matter has the perfume changed to? Why did the perfume change from a liquid to a gas?* Explain that heat is needed for liquids to become gas, but sometimes the heat in the environment is enough. Introduce the word 'evaporation' as the term used when a liquid changes to a gas.
- Ask the students to look at the pictures on Student's Book page 48. Ask: *What can you see coming from the kettle? Where has this come from? Why?* Establish that the water in the kettle is evaporating and is changing into a gas; reinforce that the steam they can see in the picture is not a gas but is made from lots of tiny water droplets in the air, so it is in fact a liquid. The water in the kettle is changing to a gas, but the water vapour (gas) is invisible. Explain that the students will learn more about water vapour in the next unit. Ask: *Does water evaporate from the lake in the photo?* Make sure that the students understand that evaporation from a water surface can happen even at everyday temperatures. Ask: *So what is the effect of heat?* (Liquids evaporate faster at higher temperatures.)

Chemistry • Topic 3 States of matter 3.5

Teaching and learning activities

- Heat up a transparent beaker (or transparent heatproof pan) of water over a gas burner. Do not fill the beaker/pan more than two-thirds full, and keep the students well away while ensuring they are still able to see. (You might want to set up a camera linked to a computer and screen.) If possible, have a dark background behind the beaker so the students can see the steam as the water gets hotter.

- When the water begins to boil, ask the students to comment on what they see. Point out that the production of steam is now great and bubbles are escaping from throughout the liquid. Ask: *What is in the bubbles?* Remind them that bubbles in a liquid are bubbles of gas, and explain that in this case the bubbles contain water vapour, or water in its gas state.

- Tell the students that when all of the liquid bubbles like this, it is because all of it is changing state. Explain that this is called boiling and it only happens when the liquid is hot enough for all of it to change state. Evaporation is different because only the part of the liquid at the surface is changing state. This can happen at much lower temperatures, but the change of state occurs much slower than boiling.

- Show the students Video C5: Boiling and steam to reiterate what happens when water boils.

- Ask the student's to look at page 49 of the Student's Book. Explain that Jamie left the three pots, each containing 100 ml of water, in three different places in the classroom for two hours then measured the volume of water again. Discuss the results shown in the table. Ask the students to discuss the questions in pairs. Ask: *What conclusions can be drawn from Jamie's results? Can you work out the total amount of evaporation?* Go from pair to pair and ask questions about Jamie's experiments: *What do his results show? What did he do to keep his test fair?*

Graded activities

1 Ask the groups to plan an investigation to test their ideas. Take feedback from the groups and review proposals. Establish whether their ideas will provide a fair test. Ask the students to make some predictions about which container the water will evaporate from the fastest. Ask them to set up their investigations, recording the details of types of containers used and the amount of water in them on page 34 of the Workbook. They should use the same volume of water in each container and put all containers in the same place. Explain that they will leave their containers until the next lesson.

2 Students should complete this activity independently once they have done the experiment.

3 Students can work in pairs to do this activity. It may be useful to tell them that they are advisors from the water authority and have them think about how they will best present their advice to a community.

Consolidate and review

- On the board, draw a diagram of two puddles evaporating. State that they both contain the same volume of water. One has a large surface area, the other has a small surface area. Ask: *Which puddle will dry up first? Why?*

- Use DVD Activity C4: Key words to consolidate and reinforce the vocabulary taught in this topic.

- Ask students to refer back to the diagram of the water cycle (Student's Book, page 43). Let them point out where evaporation is likely to occur.

Differentiation

■ All of the students should be able to set up the equipment and carry out the experiment. They should be able to correctly measure volume. Some students may struggle with the mathematics. If this is the case, help them or allow them to use a calculator to do the subtractions.

● Most of the students should be able to state what they kept the same and what they changed. They will point out that it may not be possible to do an entirely fair test as they cannot control wind and other environmental factors that could affect the rate of evaporation.

▲ Some of the students should be able to say that a smaller surface area on a lake would reduce evaporation. More able students will include other factors, such as wind shields or covers for the lake during the day, to prevent evaporation and to allow the water to condense in the cooler evenings.

Chemistry • Topic 3 States of matter 3.6

3.6 Gas to liquid

Student's Book pages 50–51
Chemistry learning objectives
- Investigate how materials change when they are heated and cooled
- Observe how water turns into steam when it is heated but on cooling the steam turns back into water.

Resources
- Workbook pages 35–36
- PCM C1: Condensation

Classroom equipment
- for the kettle demonstration (and Experiment 1): saucepan or kettle; water; large glass mirror or plate; oven gloves
- for Experiment 2: container of warm water; plastic film; ice cubes
- for Experiment 3: an empty can; a cloth; ice cubes

Scientific enquiry skills
- *Consider evidence and approach:* Identify simple trends and patterns in results and suggest explanations for some of these; explain what the evidence shows and whether it supports predictions. Communicate this clearly to others; link evidence to scientific knowledge and understanding in some contexts.

Key words
- vapour
- cools
- condensation

> ⚠ The students should be at a safe distance when water is being boiled and should not handle containers of hot water.

Scientific background

Gas is one of the three states of matter. Liquids can turn to gases and gases can change back to liquids; these are reversible changes. Gases can change back to liquids when cooled – when the heat energy decreases. The gas particles lose energy, slow down and convert to particles of liquid. This is called condensing. It happens at any temperature between the melting point and the boiling point of the material, but is greater at lower temperatures.

There are many examples where condensation and evaporation are useful. The most important situation is in the desert. Many animals and plants have adapted and become highly specialised in condensing water from the air and using it to survive. Darkling beetles live in the Namib Desert. They stand on top of sand dunes to collect the condensing water vapour from the sea fogs. The water vapour condenses on their bodies. In the Atacama Desert, people erect large nets to allow water vapour to condense. They collect it in tubes leading to a reservoir. To achieve this, they have mimicked what happens on the surface of cactus plants.

Introduction

- Ask the students: *Have you noticed what happens to some surfaces such as mirrors or saucepan lids in steamy rooms?* Let them describe what they observe and try to explain why they think this happens.
- Set up Experiments 1 and 3 (see Student's Book pages 50 and 51) so that the students can observe them from time to time during the lesson.
- Demonstrate condensation. For the demonstration, boil some water and let the steam (water vapour) hit the cold surface of a plate or mirror, held with oven gloves. Warn the students about the dangers of steam by explaining that it is extremely hot and can cause blistering or burns. Discuss the beads of water that appear on a cold surface. Ask: *What is happening?* Explain that this is condensation. The water vapour (gas) is hitting the cold mirror or tile, cooling and changing its state back to liquid water.

Chemistry • Topic 3 States of matter 3.6

Teaching and learning activities

- Turn to the Student's Book. Look at the photograph on page 50 showing condensation on a can. This is something most students should have experienced. Discuss questions 1 and 2 as a class. Make sure students realise that the water does not come from the container. If they are doubtful, demonstrate with a cold, sealed bottle or can (that does not contain water) to prove this.

- Ask the students to look at the diagrams of three different experiments on pages 50 and 51 of the Student's Book. Encourage them to ask questions about the investigations. Let the students look at questions 3 to 5 on page 51 and try to answer them. Ask for volunteers to explain their answers to the class, and take feedback from other class members.

- Discuss questions 3 to 5 and record the students' ideas on the board before moving on.

Graded activities

1 Demonstrate the three experiments detailed in the Student's Book to the class. Depending on the ability of your students, you may not need to demonstrate experiment 2, as a similar demonstration has been done already in the Teaching and learning activities. Give the students time to record their observations on page 35 of their Workbooks.

2 Encourage students to ask people who drive (primary sources) what they do when their car windows mist up. If this is not possible, they can find the information in reference books or on the internet.

3 Students can use a large diagram of the water cycle to help them complete this task. They can also refer back to Unit 3.2 where this is covered.

Consolidate and review

- Give each student a copy of PCM C1: Condensation. Ask them to write a caption for each picture using the correct scientific terms. They should draw their own examples, with captions, in the last block.

- Remind the class that evaporation and condensation are changes of state and that they are the reverse of each other. Use Workbook page 36 to informally assess understanding of the topic.

- If the class is interested, encourage them to do some research to find out how evaporation is controlled and how condensation can be used to 'harvest' water. There is some interesting work happening in Gujarat, India, where solar panels are being built over irrigation canals to provide electricity, but also to reduce evaporation from the surface of the canals and allow water to condense on the underside and run back into the canals.

Differentiation

■ All of the students should be able to record some basic observations. More able students will make detailed notes using correct scientific vocabulary.

● Most of the students should be able to state that cars have demisters that blow hot air onto the windows to prevent them from misting up. More able students will think critically about this and make some creative suggestions of their own.

▲ Some of the students should be able to state where evaporation and condensation occur in the water cycle. They should be able to give a clear presentation, including the fact that the processes are reversible and that the cycle is powered by heat from the Sun.

Chemistry • Topic 3 States of matter Consolidation

Consolidation

Student's Book page 52

Chemistry learning objectives
- Know that matter can be solid, liquid or gas.
- Investigate how materials change when they are heated and cooled.
- Know that melting is when a solid turns into a liquid and is the reverse of freezing.
- Observe how water turns into steam when it is heated but on cooling the steam turns back into water.

Resources
- DVD Activity C5: Changes of state
- Assessment Sheets C1, C2, and C3

Looking back

- Use the summary points to review the key things that the students have learned in the topic. Make up some true and false statements based on the summary points. Share these with the class and let the students decide whether the statements are true or false. If false, they should say why.
- Ask students to write three sentences about new things they learned in this topic. Let them tell their group about these things and say why they found them interesting.
- Use DVD Activity C5: Changes of state to check that the students understand and can apply what they have learned.

How well do you remember?

You may use the revision and consolidation activities on Student's Book page 52 either as a test or as an independent homework task. In either case, check the answers with the class and let the students mark their own, or each other's, work.

Some suggested answers
1. solid
2. evaporate
3. air
4. condense
5. liquid
6. melt
7. freeze
8. gas
9. reverse
10. steam

Assessment

A more formal assessment of the students' understanding of the topic can be undertaken using Assessment Sheets C1, C2 and C3. These can be completed in class or as a homework task.

Students following Cambridge Primary Science Framework will write progression tests set and supplied by Cambridge International Examinations at this level and feedback will be given regarding their achievement levels.

Assessment Sheet answers

Assessment Sheet C1
1. Solid – has a fixed shape, cannot flow and cannot be squashed; liquid – takes the shape of any container, can flow and cannot be squashed; gas – takes the shape of any container, can flow and can be squashed. [3]
2. liquid, solid, gas, solid, liquid [5]
3. Answers might include: blowing air into a balloon and seeing it expand; kites, trees and washing being blown by the wind etc. [2]

Assessment Sheet C2
1. three, liquid, solid, gas [4]
2. true, false, true [3]
3. Check students' diagrams. [3]

Assessment Sheet C3
1. Increased temperature – speed up; Less airflow – slow down; Increased surface area – speed up. [3]
2. liquid, melted, solid, freezing, evaporates [5]
3. a (tick); b (cross) [2]

Chemistry • Topic 3 States of matter Student's Book answers

Student's Book answers

pages 40–41
1. Answers will vary. Some suggested answers are: wood, plastic, paper, bricks, glass, concrete.
2. not by hand, only if they are in a container
3. air/oxygen
4. Students can do this orally.

pages 42–43
1. Students' own answers but could include: from taps, in bottles, as rain, rivers, reservoirs, lakes, oceans and so on.
2. In cold places where it has frozen and turned to ice.
3. It changes to a gas and mixes with the air.
4. Solid: snow and ice at the top of mountains
   liquid: rivers, oceans, rain and in droplets in clouds
   gas: in the air.
5. It repeats in an on-going way.

pages 44–45
1. It melts.
2. It gets wet at first on the surface, then water forms around it; as more water forms, the ice block gets smaller until it disappears and there is only a puddle of water left.
3. No, where it is warmer it will melt faster; larger blocks will take longer to melt than smaller blocks.
4. Examples could include: chocolate, butter, margarine, wax, ice cream.
5. Students give their own opinions. In many cases butter will melt before ice because it is 'less solid' to start with. Similarly, the wax will melt more slowly than the butter because it is designed to withstand some heat before melting.

pages 46–47
1. Students' own explanations.
2. Water, molten chocolate, jelly, molten wax and so on.
3. No, they do not. Some are solid at room temperature, others have to be supercooled before they will solidify.
4. The frozen matter (solid) is heating up and melting.
5. Student's own opinions, but should include cooking and baking, cooling objects, preserving food and so on.

pages 48–49
1. heat
2. The water in the kettle as it is being heated more vigorously and uniformly.
3. Jamie is investigating to find out how much water evaporates from differently shaped containers. He records the volume of water at the start (placing the same amount in each container), leaves the containers and measures the water again. He subtracts the amount left from how much he started with to find out how much evaporated from each container.
4. It would slow down the rate of evaporation as there would be less heat. (Cold air is denser and thus more saturated than warm air, so it absorbs less vapour.)

pages 50–51
1. water
2. the air
3. Students' own predictions, but they should include the fact that water droplets will condense on the surfaces.
4. The apparatus used, the volumes of water involved, the amount of heat applied, the temperature of the substance to start with.
5. Experiment 1: under the plastic film; Experiment 2: on the cold plate; Experiment 3: on the outside of the can. In all cases the water vapour comes from the air.

Physics • Topic 4 Sound

4.1 How sounds are made

Student's Book pages 53–55
Physics learning objective
- Explore how sounds are made when objects, materials or air vibrate and learn to measure the volume of sound in decibels with a sound level meter.

Resources
- Workbook pages 37–40

Classroom equipment
- a small bell
- for each group (Activity 2): hollow cardboard or plastic tube 3–5 cm in diameter, thin plastic film, elastic band, grains of rice
- for each group (Activity 3): plastic bottle, plastic film, elastic band, a small candle, matches, scissors
- pens and paper
- scissors
- rulers and coloured pens for drawing graphs

Scientific enquiry skills
- *Ideas and evidence:* Collect evidence in a variety of contexts.
- *Obtain and present evidence:* Make relevant observations and comparisons in a variety of contexts; present results in drawings, bar charts and tables.
- *Consider evidence and approach:* Explain what the evidence shows and whether it supports predictions. Communicate this clearly to others.

Key words
- sounds
- vibration
- vibrate

> ⚠ Supervise students as they work with the air column and candle flame. Make sure they keep the bottle a safe distance from the flame. Also make sure they work carefully with scissors.

Scientific background

Vibrations make sounds. Sound needs a medium (solid, liquid or gas) in order for it to be transmitted (to travel). Sound is transmitted when molecules vibrate and cause the molecules next to them to start vibrating as well. In this unit we look at how sound travels through air. Students will explore how sound travels through solids and liquids in Unit 4.3.

Our ears sense sound energy in the form of vibrations. Air inside the ear canal makes the eardrum vibrate. The vibrations of the eardrum are transmitted through the internal structure of the ear and activate the auditory nerve. The vibrations are changed to electrical signals that are transmitted to the brain.

The human voice is made by breathing air over our vocal cords, causing them to vibrate. When someone talks loudly or shouts close to the tube in the experiment on Workbook page 39, the sound vibrations travel through the air. They make the plastic film stretched across the top vibrate; this, in turn, makes the rice grains on top of the film jump. If the volume of sound gets louder the vibrations get bigger, so the film vibrates more, making the rice jump higher.

Take care not to confuse the *pitch* of a sound with its *volume*. The rice is likely to bounce more in response to a lower-pitched sound than to a higher-pitched one. If the students observe this, you should encourage them to make their observations based on louder and quieter sounds all made at the same pitch.

The 'sound cannon' experiment on Workbook page 40 shows how sound causes the air inside the bottle to vibrate strongly enough to make the candle flame flicker (or even to blow it out).

Introduction

- Tell the students to sit quietly and listen. Ask: *What noises can you hear in the classroom?* Take feedback and list on the board what the students can hear. Ask: *Can you explain how sound reaches your ears?* Take some responses. You may like to do activity 1 on Student's Book page 54 before you deal with the scientific concepts in this unit.

- Ask the students to think about and then discuss how they make sounds with their voices. Ask for volunteers to demonstrate how speaking makes the air move (vibrate). Tell the students to put a

Physics • Topic 4 Sound 4.1

hand against their throat and to make a series of noises, starting low and getting higher, to feel the vibrations.

Teaching and learning activities

- Turn to Student's Book page 54. Explain that sound is made by vibrations. Look at the images on the page and discuss questions 1 and 2 with the class.
- Remind the students that they felt vibrations in their throats when they made sounds with their voices. Repeat the experiment and use the text in the book to explain how we make and hear sounds.
- Ask the students to work in small groups to carry out and observe the activities in which vibrations make sounds. (Alternatively, demonstrate these if you prefer.) Possible activities include: plucking an elastic band; twanging a ruler on the desk; hitting a surface with a stick; carefully touching the speaker of a stereo system while music is being played; watching a mobile phone ring when it is switched to vibrate mode. Ask the students to talk about their observations and identify what is vibrating to produce the sound. They should draw a diagram of one of the activities, making sure to identify the vibrating part.

Graded activities

1 Explain to the class that they are going to do a survey outside the classroom to find out what sounds they can hear. Direct them to Workbook pages 37–38 and give each group or pair an area in which to sit quietly for five minutes and listen to the sounds around them. They should make a rough list of the sounds they hear. Return to the classroom and let the students complete the Workbook activities.

2 Give each group the equipment they need. The students should stretch plastic film tightly over the top of a tube and then place a few grains of rice onto the film. Tell the students to talk loudly while their head is very near the bottom of the tube and watch what happens to the rice. Tell them to talk more quietly, and also to shout. Ask: *What difference does the loudness of your voice make to the grains of rice? What is making the grains of rice bounce?* (The plastic film is moving because it is receiving vibrations from the sound of the students' voices.)

3 Hand out the equipment to each group and supervise them as they read through and carry out the instructions. Make sure they work safely with the scissors and the flame. Discuss the results and check that the students can draw a diagram to show what happened. Some students may not be able to blow out the flame because they are holding the tube too far away. Encourage them to move the tube closer and try again.

Consolidate and review

- Spend some time discussing what the students observed and learned in this unit. Talk about the experiments. Ask: *Why do louder sounds make bigger vibrations?* (Because there is more energy in the sound.) Ask the students to explain in their own words what causes the rice to jump about in response to loud and quiet sounds.
- Remind the students that their ears each contain an eardrum, a membrane that behaves in the same way as the film on the jar. Now discuss what students would hear and feel if they experienced a very loud sound. Ask what effects very loud sounds could have on the students' ears.

Differentiation

■ All of the students should be able to complete the survey and classify and tally the sounds. They should be able to draw a bar graph; assist any students who find this difficult. Some students may struggle to read and interpret the given graph because they do not read the scale properly. Ask leading questions to help them make sense of the data.

● Most of the students should know that loud sounds produce observable vibrations. They should know that sound energy is changed into vibrations, or movement energy.

▲ Some of the students should be able to read and follow the instructions without help. They will explain why the flame moved or went out in terms of vibrations moving through the air. They should be able to draw clear, labelled diagrams showing how vibrations move down the tube to the flame and how the movement of air affects the flame.

Physics • Topic 4 Sound 4.2

4.2 Measuring sound

Student's Book pages 56–57

Physics learning objective

- Explore how sounds are made when objects, materials or air vibrate and learn to measure the volume of sound in decibels with a sound level meter.

Resources

- Workbook pages 41–45

Classroom equipment

- sound level meter or mobile phone/tablet app
- apparatus for making sounds as necessary
- pens and pencils

Scientific enquiry skills

- *Plan investigative work:* Suggest questions that can be tested and make predictions; communicate these; design a fair test and plan how to collect sufficient evidence; choose apparatus and decide what to measure.
- *Obtain and present evidence:* Begin to think about the need for repeated measurements of, for example, length.
- *Consider evidence and approach:* Identify simple trends and patterns in results and suggest explanations for some of these.

Key words

- volume
- sound level meter
- decibel

Note: most modern mobile phones and tablets have built-in microphones so they can be used to record sounds. If a sound meter is not available you can download special applications (apps) that allow you to use the phone as a sound level meter.

> ⚠ Make sure students work responsibly with all electronic equipment.

Scientific background

The students will be familiar with the volume control on radio and television sets. The volume or loudness of a sound can be measured. The decibel scale is used to measure sound and noise levels in units called decibels (dB). The scale is logarithmic and every increase of 10 decibels means that the sound level has increased ten times. The lowest sound that can be detected by the human ear is classified as 0 dB.

Handheld sound level meters are used to record sounds and to calculate their intensity in decibels. Today you can download mobile apps that allow you to use your phone or tablet computer as a sound level meter.

In general, the greater the volume of sound hitting the eardrum, the greater the force the sound creates. It follows that the greater the force, the greater the damage to the nerves. Damage to hearing can be caused by intense sound waves but also by repeated exposure to loud sounds over a period of time. Repeated exposure to loud music on headphones has been shown to damage hearing.

Introduction

- Ask the class to say what the difference is between a pleasant sound and a noise. What sounds do they think are particularly noisy? What sounds are unpleasant?
- Explain that sounds can be soft or loud and that we call the loudness of a sound its volume. Demonstrate how to change the volume of a device using the volume control (you could use a mobile phone to do this, or a portable music device).
- Explain that scientists use measurements to compare different levels of sound. Use the diagram of the decibel scale on Student's Book page 56 to introduce the units. Discuss the sounds shown on the scale and pay attention to the levels of sound along the bottom. Discuss questions 1 to 3 as a class. Ask the students to suggest where the noise level of their classroom fits on the scale.

Physics • Topic 4 Sound 4.2

Teaching and learning activities

- Explain what a sound level meter is and show the class if you have one. If not, make sure you have some kind of application available to use. Answer questions 4 and 5 as a class.
- Demonstrate the use of a sound level meter (or app) by measuring the sound level of one person clapping their hands, three people clapping their hands and the whole class clapping together. Discuss where the different levels fit on the decibel scale.
- Spend some time allowing the students to experience the equipment and use it to measure different sound levels. It is important that they can use the device before they attempt the practical activities.

Graded activities

1 Let the students work in pairs to complete the activity. Make sure they record the sound levels and both readings. This is an important step as it allows them to see that results may vary and that repeated measurements are used in science to gain an accurate or average result. Different readings may be the result of different equipment, the person measuring and/or the environmental conditions.

2 Let the students work in small groups to plan this investigation. Allow them to work through questions 1 to 5 and then review their ideas and approve their plans before they start the investigation.

3 Students should refer to the information on Workbook page 45. They can do this activity independently as an additional classroom activity, or they can complete it at home. Using secondary sources will help them to develop scientific literacy skills, and interpreting the information will encourage them to think critically and apply what they have learned to a real-world context.

Consolidate and review

- Use Workbook page 44 to classify sounds by volume and to consolidate work done in this unit. Let the students compare their completed sheets and justify their choices, particularly if these are different. For some of the sounds, they could check their answers using the sound level meter.
- Ask the students to make leaflets to warn of the dangers of loud sounds.
- Let students work in groups to write some sound safety rules for the use of headphones. Share the ideas with the class.

Differentiation

■ All of the students should be able to use the sound level meter to measure and record sounds in decibels. They should be able to explain why their results may differ slightly. More able students will give clear answers explaining different factors that could result in different measurements.

● Most of the students should be able to plan a fair test. Some students may struggle to choose apparatus and decide what to measure. Refer them back to their question and what they are investigating to help them make these decisions. More able students should realise and express clearly that the volume of sound depends on the distance of the source of the sound from the object hearing the sound.

▲ Some of the students should be able to provide at least one situation in which it might be useful to measure sound levels. They will give detailed and well-reasoned replies referring to environmental noise levels as well as occupational health and safety.

Physics • Topic 4 Sound 4.3

4.3 Sound travels through different materials

Student's Book pages 58–59

Physics learning objective
- Investigate how sound travels through different materials to the ear.

Resources
- Workbook pages 46–48
- Video P1: Whale songs

Classroom equipment
- selection of different sized and shaped disposable cups (paper, polystyrene and plastic), tins, lengths of different materials that can be used as string (fishing line, thread, wool, thin rope, string), paperclips (to use as stoppers and prevent string pulling through cups), something sharp to make holes in the cups/tins
- balloons, plastic bottles, water, basins, small stones

Scientific enquiry skills
- *Ideas and evidence:* Collect evidence in a variety of contexts; test an idea or prediction based on scientific knowledge and understanding.
- *Plan investigative work:* Suggest questions that can be tested and make predictions; communicate these; design a fair test and plan how to collect sufficient evidence; choose apparatus and decide what to measure.
- *Consider evidence and approach:* Explain what the evidence shows and whether it supports predictions. Communicate this clearly to others; link evidence to scientific knowledge and understanding in some contexts.

Key words
- source
- medium
- metres per second

⚠ Supervise students while they are making holes in cups/tins. When they are working with water, remind them that spillages can make the floor slippery, and make sure they mop up any spills immediately.

Scientific background

Sound travels in longitudinal waves made by objects that vibrate. As discussed in Unit 4.1, sound needs a medium in order to travel; this can be solid, liquid or gas. Sound travels through the air at about 330 metres per second (m/s). When the molecules are closely packed together, as in a liquid or solid, sound can travel faster and better. Sound travels through steel at 3600 m/s. Sonar equipment uses the ability of sound to travel through liquid. Sound cannot travel through a vacuum as there are no air particles to vibrate. In space, where there is no atmosphere, sound cannot be generated.

When someone speaks into a paper-cup telephone, the sound is transmitted into the structure of the cup, including the base. The bottom of the cup acts as a diaphragm and vibrates with the sound of the speaker's voice. As the bottom of the cup vibrates, it transmits the vibrations into the taut string. The sound travels along the string as a longitudinal wave and vibrates the bottom of the receiving cup. The cup transmits the sound into the air around the listener's ear, so they can hear the speaker. Because the sound travels better through solids than through air, the users can speak across large distances.

Introduction

- Remind the class that sound can travel through air. Ask the students to tell you how they know this from their own observations. Remind them that air is a gas and that if sound can travel through air, it can also travel through other gases.
- Ask the students if they think sound can travel through solids. Let them give some responses. If they say yes, ask them how they know this. If they say no, ask them to justify their answer. Allow the students to take turns to listen to each other tapping on the desk. Point out that with their ear against the desk no air can reach it, so the vibrations must be coming from the desk itself.

Physics • Topic 4 Sound 4.3

- Ask the class if they think sound can travel through liquids. Again, let them say why they decided and why they know this.

Teaching and learning activities

- Turn to Student's Book page 58. Use the airplane example to reiterate that sound can travel through air.
- Talk about different solids (wood, brick, concrete, glass, and so on). Which ones are good at transmitting sound? Make sure students realise that not all solids are good at transmitting sound.
- Play Video P1: Whale songs to the class. Explain that whales can hear each other over very long distances. The sounds are recorded underwater, but usually some distance from the whales, which shows that the sound is able to travel through water.
- Briefly explain that sound travels faster through liquids than through air because the vibrations cannot spread out so much. Explain that sound travels even faster through solids as the vibrations can spread out even less.

Graded activities

1 The students use Workbook pages 46 and 47 to design and make a string telephone. Allow them to select the materials to make their telephones. They need to make sure the string doesn't slip through the holes in the cups (they can use a paperclip or a small stick as a stopper) and to keep the string tight in order for sounds to be transmitted. Make sure they realise, or work out, that they cannot have their fingers or other objects touching the string. You will need to spend some time in the playground for the students to test their telephones. Remind them to speak normally or whisper rather than shout, so they know that the phone is transmitting the sound (rather than a loud sound being transmitted through air).

2 Using Workbook page 48, students must evaluate two experiments and predict the outcomes based on what they already know about sound and sound transmission. Let them discuss the experiments in pairs or groups, but have them complete the table independently. Allow some time for them to do their experiment in class, if possible; alternatively, ask them to try it at home.

3 Students can carry out this research in small groups. Allow interested students to explore the topic in more depth, considering ultrasound and other medical technology if they raise this. Allow the groups time to present their findings to the class.

Consolidate and review

- Spend some time talking about and reviewing the string telephone activity. Make sure students can answer questions such as: *What makes a string telephone work? What is making the vibrations? In what way are the vibrations being transmitted? Could you improve the telephone you made? Why would the improvements make it better?* Make sure the students understand that neither landline nor mobile telephones work like this.
- Ask the students to make a concept map summarising what they have learned about sound so far. They should do this in their books as they will add to it later in the topic.

Differentiation

■ All of the students should be able to design and make a string telephone and explain how it works. More able students will think more critically about materials and how well they absorb or transmit sound and use this knowledge to design the most effective system.

● Most of the students should be able to work out what they are doing. Some students may struggle to give details to complete the table. Encourage them to discuss their ideas and ask questions to assist them.

▲ Some of the students should be able to find out what sonar is and how it is used. They should be able to explain the two types of sonar and how they work, giving clear and detailed explanations with supporting evidence and diagrams.

Physics • Topic 4 Sound 4.4

4.4 Reducing sound levels

Student's Book pages 60–61

Physics learning objective
- Investigate how some materials are effective in preventing sound from travelling through them.

Resources
- Workbook page 49
- Slideshow P1: Using ear protection

Classroom equipment
- samples of cheap earplugs to show the class
- for each group: materials for making ear protectors – cups (ideally round), could be plastic food containers, drinking cups (if they are big enough) or food bowls; cotton wool, tissue paper, foam or fabric

Scientific enquiry skills
- *Ideas and evidence:* Collect evidence in a variety of contexts; test an idea or prediction based on scientific knowledge and understanding.
- *Plan investigative work:* Suggest questions that can be tested and make predictions; communicate these; design a fair test and plan how to collect sufficient evidence; choose apparatus and decide what to measure.
- *Obtain and present evidence:* Begin to think about the need for repeated measurements of, for example, length.
- *Consider evidence and approach:* Explain what the evidence shows and whether it supports predictions. Communicate this clearly to others; link evidence to scientific knowledge and understanding in some contexts.

Key word
- soundproof

Scientific background

Exposure to loud sounds can lead to hearing damage or loss. Continual exposure to a noise level of more than 85 dB can lead to permanent hearing damage. The best way to protect against hearing damage is to prevent sound waves from entering the ears. There are many methods of doing this: for example, earplugs (usually made of foam or rubber) are placed inside the ear; ear protectors are cups (like headphone cups) that fit over the ears – they are filled with foam and other materials that cut down or prevent the transmission of sound, stopping the sound from entering the ears.

Introduction

- Start the lesson by playing some music or sounds to the class. Ask the students to put their hands over their ears. Ask: *What do you notice?* Students should compare qualitatively what they can hear with nothing over their ears, with their hands over their ears and, if available, with some earplugs or ear protectors on. Discuss these differences in terms of the sound energy travelling to their ears.

- Ask the students to make a list of unpleasant or annoying sounds. Then ask them to suggest what they could use to block out these sounds more effectively than with their own hands. List their suggestions on the board; you will refer back to these later.

- Show the class the earplugs you have brought to class. Ask when you might need to wear these. Discuss what they are made of and how they work.

Teaching and learning activities

- Turn to Student's Book page 60. Look at the photograph of the recording studio and discuss questions 1 and 2 as a class. Point out some of the insulating materials used in a recording studio. Explain that the musician normally wears a set of earphones that he or she uses to listen to the music while cutting out any other sounds.

- Explain that some people use ear protection when they do their jobs. Ask: *What does the ear protection look like? What kinds of loud sounds would require the use of ear protection? Why is it important to wear ear protection when you are in a noisy environment?*

Physics • Topic 4 Sound 4.4

- Discuss the image of the road drill operator on Student's Book page 61 and examine the ear protectors in the photographs. Answer questions 3–5 as a class.
- Show Slideshow P1: Using ear protection. For each slide, let the students identify the source of the unwanted sound, suggest where it would fall on the decibel scale and say how the worker is protecting their hearing.

Graded activities

1 Ask the students to work in pairs to evaluate the ear protectors shown in the photographs. Encourage them to make a labelled sketch to show what materials they think are used to make them. If possible, show the class a real pair of ear protectors.

2 Let the students work in pairs or small groups to design, make and test three different sets of ear protectors. The cups could be plastic food containers, drinking cups (if they are big enough) or food bowls. Ideally they should be round. Possible materials include cotton wool, tissue paper, foam or fabric. The testing procedure should be repeated two or three times to gather more evidence. Groups should also gather data without ear protectors in order to make a comparison. Students should complete question 2 of Worksheet page 49 on their own.

3 Before doing this activity students can review the slideshow to refresh their memories, but they should also do some additional research either by asking adults in the community, reading sources or using the internet

Consolidate and review

- Ask each group to write a number of noisy situations on cards. Let them pass these to another group and ask them to rank these from most to least noisy.
- Next, let the students say which of these situations would require ear protection and let them suggest what these might be.
- Share the lists the students developed in Activity 3. Let them group the activities by their potential to damage hearing. They should choose two or three groups and place the activities in these based on what they know about the sound levels.
- Ask the students to add to their concept maps any new information they have learned about sound.

Differentiation

■ All of the students should be able to give a basic explanation and to say that the ear protectors contain materials that block sound, even if they cannot name specific materials. More able students should be able to identify at least one or two materials used to make the ear protectors.

● Most of the students will design and carry out fair tests using a range of effective insulating materials. They will be able to explain that the materials absorb sound and stop it reaching their ears. Some students will choose unsuitable materials to fill the cups. This is fine as long as they realise that the materials do not work to block sound.

▲ Some of the students will do their own research and add interesting and varied examples.

61

4.5 Soundproofing materials

Student's Book pages 62–63

Physics learning objective
- Investigate how some materials are effective in preventing sound from travelling through them.

Resources
- Workbook pages 50–53

Classroom equipment
- for each group: boxes, e.g. photocopier paper or shoe box, a range of materials, e.g. card, paper, foil, fabric, bubble wrap, foam, a buzzer or alarm clock, sound level meter

Scientific enquiry skills
- *Ideas and evidence:* Collect evidence in a variety of contexts; test an idea or prediction based on scientific knowledge and understanding.
- *Plan investigative work:* Suggest questions that can be tested and make predictions; communicate these; design a fair test and plan how to collect sufficient evidence; choose apparatus and decide what to measure.
- *Obtain and present evidence:* Begin to think about the need for repeated measurements of, for example, length.
- *Consider evidence and approach:* Explain what the evidence shows and whether it supports predictions. Communicate this clearly to others; link evidence to scientific knowledge and understanding in some contexts.

Key words
- **transmission**
- **muffle**

⚠️ Do not let students experiment with toxic or hazardous materials.

Scientific background

Some materials allow sound to travel through them very easily. Hard solids such as wood and metals are good at transmitting sounds. Other materials, especially soft ones such as foam or cotton wool, absorb or dampen sound, effectively preventing it from travelling further. When these materials are combined with air, which is a poor transmitter of sound, or other gases, they work more effectively. So, for example, egg-box-shaped foam is more effective as a soundproofing layer than flat sheets of foam, as the egg-box structure contains large air spaces.

Introduction

- Ask the class a few questions to recap what they learned about stopping sound transmission in the previous lesson. For example: *When do we need to stop sound from travelling to our ears? Do all materials reduce the sound level? Which materials work best?*
- Turn to Student's Book page 62. Look at the diagram and let the students suggest answers to the questions. Explain the way soundproofing works with reference to the text on the page.
- Discuss the materials used for soundproofing and the way they work (basically, they absorb vibrations).

Teaching and learning activities

- In this lesson, the graded activities will effectively be the main teaching and learning activities. Discuss with the class the different activities and what is required. Activity 1 is fairly straightforward and will require little input. For Activity 2, explain to the students that they will place the buzzer in the cardboard box with the battery and switch outside. They should connect the circuit and measure the loudness of the buzzer. They then pack a sound insulation material around the buzzer before testing the sound level a second time. The students should test a range of materials to try to determine which sort of material works the best for soundproofing. Students should write down their results in the table on Workbook page 51. For Activity 3, make sure the students identify where noise transmission is a problem before they add soundproofing solutions.

Physics • Topic 4 Sound 4.5

Graded activities

1 Let the students complete this activity on their own. This task will allow them to predict results and select suitable materials for soundproofing in the other two activities.

2 Students should work in groups to plan an investigation into how different insulating materials affect the loudness of the sound from an electric buzzer. They should plan a fair test and plan to collect reliable evidence. They could collect results using a sound level (decibel) meter to get quantitative results, if one is available. To avoid the noise from one group interfering with the others, try to separate the groups as much as possible, making use of other rooms if possible.

3 This activity requires the students to apply the scientific knowledge they have developed in this unit (and the previous one) to solve a real-life problem related to soundproofing. Allow the students to talk about and share their ideas, but have them all complete the diagrams on Workbook page 53 independently.

Consolidate and review

- Discuss the soundproofing activities in class. Students should discuss and compare their results as they may have come to different conclusions. Encourage them to discuss results in terms of the type of material that did not let the sound through very well, e.g. 'The bubble wrap was best because it contains air and air is a poor sound transporter'; 'The foil was the noisiest as it does not contain any air.'

- In order to rank and informally measure sound levels, the students could produce comparative scales of loudness, e.g. 'as quiet as a sniff', 'as loud as a door slamming' (and scales in between). Let them share their scales as a class and allow discussion to resolve any inconsistencies or disagreements.

- Students could survey sound in the school building and grounds to find where the noisy areas are. Once they have done this, they could draw up a labelled plan showing how the school could reduce the noise levels.

- Ask the students to add to their sound concept maps any new information they have learned.

Differentiation

■ All of the students should be able to rank the materials and be able to justify their choices (even if they are based on inaccuracies). More able students may be more technically inclined and will want to find out the correct rankings.

● Most of the students will plan a fair test, using the same equipment, the same thickness of insulation, and measuring/listening the same distance away. They will repeat readings to improve the reliability of their evidence and record their results in a table. More able students will identify unusual results, calculate the average value for each different material and present their results as a column graph. They will use their results to draw conclusions about the best sorts of materials for sound insulation.

▲ Some of the students should be able to make some suggestions for absorbing sound. They will provide very detailed diagrams with specifications for using specific materials in different places.

Physics • Topic 4 Sound 4.6

4.6 Musical instruments

Student's Book pages 64–65
Physics learning objective
- Explore how sounds are made when objects, materials or air vibrate and learn to measure the volume of sound in decibels with a sound level meter.

Resources
- Workbook pages 54 and 55
- Video P2: Musical instruments
- DVD Activity P1: How different instruments are played

Classroom equipment
- samples of musical instruments, if available
- books and CD-ROMs about music and instruments

Scientific enquiry skills
- *Ideas and evidence:* Collect evidence in a variety of contexts; test an idea or prediction based on scientific knowledge and understanding.

Key words
- sound
- vibrate

⚠️ Students should handle musical instruments with care.

Scientific background

Sounds are produced by vibrations. Vibrations can be produced in many ways, and the characteristics of the sounds produced depend on the material that is vibrating and the way it is made to vibrate. Instruments that have strings, for example, produce sounds because the strings vibrate. The sound of a piano, however, is very different from that of a violin and different again from that of a guitar, partly because the way that the vibrations are caused is different. Other types of instrument have different vibrating parts, each producing a characteristic type of sound.

Stringed instruments make a sound when their strings are plucked or strummed because the strings vibrate and the vibrations are transferred to the air. The sound of a wind instrument comes when we blow air into it, causing the air inside to vibrate. Percussion instruments vibrate when they are struck. The human voice is made by breathing air over our vocal cords, causing them to vibrate; it is like a cross between a string and a wind instrument.

Musical instruments work by amplifying vibrations. The vibrations can be produced by blowing air, striking the instrument or plucking a string. The body of the instrument resonates and amplifies the noise, making it louder.

Introduction

- Ask the students: *Do you know anyone who plays a musical instrument? What kind of instrument is it? What makes it produce a sound?* Show the students Video P2: Musical instruments, then ask them to describe and explain how each instrument is played.

- Let the students watch and listen to someone playing a musical instrument for a few minutes. Invite the students to make comments about what they hear and to ask questions. The musician should show the students the instrument and answer their questions.

Teaching and learning activities

- Turn to Student's Book pages 64 and 65. Let the students work in pairs to read the information and answer the questions. Have a feedback session with the whole class.

- With the help of the students, demonstrate using percussion instruments and establish that the sounds are generated through hitting. Emphasise that 'percussion' means the playing of music by striking instruments with objects such as sticks. If possible, demonstrate wind instruments, for example a recorder, and stringed instruments, such as a guitar or piano. Discuss the way the sounds are made. Encourage the students to think and talk about what part of each instrument is vibrating.

Physics • Topic **4** Sound 4.6

When looking at instruments with sound boxes, e.g. stringed instruments, ask: *Why do you think the strings have been placed over a hollow box?*

Graded activities

1 Let the students work in pairs to model the instruments and make sounds with them, using Workbook page 54 to generate ideas. Observe the students as they work and ask questions to make sure they know what is vibrating and what is causing the vibration in each case. Allow the students to share their own examples with the class and let the others say what is vibrating and what is making it vibrate in each model.

2 Let the students complete this activity on their own, using Workbook page 55. Collect their work and check it to make sure they understand the concepts. Alternatively, provide model answers and let the students check each other's work in groups.

3 Students can work in pairs or small groups to do the research and prepare their presentations.

Consolidate and review

- Give the groups time to give their presentations. Let the others take notes and ask questions after each one.
- Show the class pictures of different instruments and let them say how they make sounds. Present some unfamiliar instruments, such as an accordion or traditional instruments, and challenge them to describe how they are played and how they make sounds.
- Use DVD Activity P1: How different instruments are played, to reinforce the concepts.
- Ask the students to add to their concept maps any additional information they think is relevant.

Differentiation

■ All of the students should be able to model the instruments and use them to produce sounds. They will be able to complete the table correctly. Some students will struggle to find creative examples of their own.

● Most of the students should be able to complete the fact files with some level of detail and classify the instruments by type.

▲ Some of the students will be able to produce a presentation with little or no help. A few students may need some guidance so they do not choose an instrument that is too complex, e.g. a synthesizer. This is a good opportunity for most students to research instruments from other cultures.

65

Physics • Topic 4 Sound 4.7

4.7 Pitch

Student's Book pages 66–67

Physics learning objective
- Investigate the way pitch describes how high or low a sound is and that high and low sounds can be loud or soft. Secondary sources can be used.

Resources
- Workbook pages 56 and 57
- Audio clip P1: High and low pitch
- Video P3: Music

Classroom equipment
- plastic rulers

Scientific enquiry skills
- *Ideas and evidence:* Collect evidence in a variety of contexts; test an idea of prediction based on scientific knowledge and understanding.
- *Obtain and present evidence:* Make relevant observations and comparisons in a variety of contexts.
- *Consider evidence and approach:* Identify simple trends and patterns in results and suggest explanations for some of these.

Key words
- pitch
- high-pitched
- low-pitched

⚠ Make sure students don't over-bend their rulers and break them.

Scientific background

Changing the length of the vibrating material changes the pitch of a sound. A short and thin length will create a high-pitched note. Increasing the length or the thickness will produce a lower-pitched note. The faster an object vibrates, the higher the pitch of the sound. The pitch of a sound generated by a vibrating object is related to its size. The loudness of a sound depends on the amount of energy carried by the sound. Sound can be loud or soft without changing pitch.

We can only hear a limited amount of the sound energy that surrounds us. Very low-pitched and very high-pitched sounds are outside our hearing range. Animals have a much wider range of hearing. Elephants make and can hear very low sounds. Many animals, including bats, make and hear very high sounds.

Sound waves can be shown on a special device called an oscilloscope. The loudness and pitch of a sound determine what the sound wave on the screen will look like. A loud sound produces a large (high) wave. A soft sound will produce a small (low) wave. High sounds produce waves that are short and close together, and low sounds produce waves that are long and spread out. (The students do not need to be able to interpret sound wave diagrams. This information is here as scientific background only.)

Introduction

- Introduce the terms 'pitch' – how high or low a sound is – and 'loudness'. Explain that loudness depends on the size of vibrations that make the sound – the bigger the vibrations (the bigger the amplitude) the louder the sound. Pitch is determined by the speed of the vibrations – the faster the vibrations the higher the note. This is demonstrated by plucking a long string and a short string and observing that the vibrations are quicker in the short string. If this is difficult to see, try attaching a ping-pong ball to a length of cotton and resting the ball on a plucked string. The difference in the speed of vibrations can be observed by the banging of the ball.

- Demonstrate a range of musical instruments to the students (or arrange for the school music teacher to do so). Demonstrate the way each instrument makes low and high notes and loud and quiet notes. (If any students play an instrument, ask them if they would like to demonstrate to the rest of the class.) Note that you will explore how to change the pitch in instruments in the next lesson, so focus rather on the high and low sounds at this stage.

Physics • Topic 4 Sound 4.7

Teaching and learning activities

- Play Audio clip P1. Let the students take turns to identify the sounds and to say whether they are high or low pitched sounds. Change the volume of the player to make the point that a sound of the same pitch can be loud or soft and that volume does not change the pitch. For example, a soft whine is just as high pitched as a loud whine.
- Turn to Student's Book pages 66 and 67. Ask the students to read silently through the text before discussing questions 1 to 3.
- Play Video P3: Music. Ask the students to describe the sounds in terms of both pitch and volume.

Graded activities

It is recommended that the students should attempt all three activities and work in mixed ability groups. Differentiation should be through the level of support the students receive as they work on the activity, as well as by outcome (please see guidance in the 'Differentiation' box opposite).

1 Allow the students to experiment with their rulers and then discuss the questions on Workbook page 56 as a class. Make sure the students realise that the sound stops when the ruler stops moving (in other words, when the vibrations stop).

2 Let the students attempt the wordsearch on Workbook page 57 their own. This will reinforce some of the key words they have learned so far in this topic and will also draw upon their literacy skills.

3 Students who have studied music may already know the answer to this question. Encourage them to share what they know with the class. Provide reference books and/or CD-ROM or internet access so students can read about different terms used to describe sounds.

Consolidate and review

- Discuss the ruler activity as a class. Ask: *What did you do to make a sound with the ruler? What caused the sound to start? What made the sound stop? Could you make the sounds softer or louder? Explain how you could do this.*
- Ask for volunteers to make a sound with a ruler. Have another student describe the volume and pitch of the sound.
- Let students add to their concept map about sound.

Differentiation

■ All of the students should be able to do the task and to explain their observations in simple terms. Some students may have difficulty distinguishing between pitch and volume. Remind them that the pitch is not related to how loud or soft a sound is. Repeat some of the sounds from the audio clip at low and high volume to make the point again.

● Most of the students should be able to independently find the words in the wordsearch. Less able students may need additional help either from the teacher or from more able students in their group.

▲ Some of the students should be able to complete the activity with minimal help, they will help less able students in the group with the research. Check that all of the students are able to explain the term 'tone' in their own words, as well as how tone differs from volume and pitch. Ensure they do not just plagiarise sources; ask questions to make sure they understand the terms.

Physics • Topic 4 Sound 4.8

4.8 Changing the pitch of a musical instrument

Student's Book pages 68–69

Physics learning objective
- Explore how pitch can be changed in musical instruments in a range of ways.

Resources
- Workbook page 58
- Video P2: Musical instruments
- Video P4: Playing a guitar

Classroom equipment
- drinking straws
- for demonstration: wooden block with three nails knocked into it and an elastic band, as per diagram on page 68 of the Student's Book
- a selection of musical instruments, if possible: drums of various sizes, piano, xylophone, etc.

Scientific enquiry skills
- *Ideas and evidence:* Collect evidence in a variety of contexts; test an idea of prediction based on scientific knowledge and understanding.
- *Obtain and present evidence:* Make relevant observations and comparisons in a variety of contexts.
- *Consider evidence and approach:* Identify simple trends and patterns in results and suggest explanations for some of these.

Key words
- **pitch**
- **vibrate**

⚠️ If students are working with musical instruments, make sure they handle them carefully and responsibly. When they are playing music with glass bottles, make sure they don't hit the bottles too hard as they may break. Also, remind them to clean up any water spillage immediately.

Scientific background

Different families of instruments exhibit a range of pitch. The piano is remarkable in that it has a very wide range. The two families that are easiest to understand are the woodwind and the strings. The instruments in each family change in size, but the shapes of the instruments are very similar. The length of the woodwind instruments increases from the piccolo to the bassoon. The strings similarly increase in size from the violin to the double bass. The brass and percussion instruments are more difficult to understand if the students do not have experience of playing them.

The students will have seen that in the orchestra the instruments get bigger in all three dimensions. It is relatively easy to study change of pitch in some percussion instruments. The xylophone is an ideal instrument for students to investigate and use to study controlling variables.

Introduction
- Play Video P2: Musical instruments again. Discuss how the musicians are changing the pitch of the different instruments and compare the pitch of different instruments in general.
- Turn to Student's Book page 68. Let students answer questions 1 and 2 orally before using the model guitar you have made to demonstrate that each length of elastic produces notes of different pitch. Ask them if their answers were correct.
- Let the students work in pairs to read through the rest of the information in the Student's Book and answer the remaining questions.

Teaching and learning activities
- Show the students drums of various sizes and ask them to hit the drums to demonstrate the range of sounds they can make. Ensure that they observe that the characteristics of the sound depend on the size of the drum and where it is struck. Explain that

Physics • Topic 4 Sound 4.8

in an orchestra or a band, musicians want to get the same sound from the instrument, so the instrument must always be played in the same way. Ask the students why comparing two drums of different sizes may not be a fair test and list their answers.

- Demonstrate high and low pitch on the piano and ask the students to try to sing to match the note by singing 'high' or 'low'. When they are confident, make the intervals smaller and ask them to compare the notes by singing 'higher' and 'lower', as appropriate.

- Introduce the xylophone and demonstrate how the sounds are generated. Group the students and allow them to explore the xylophone and the beaters. Then ask the following questions (it may be helpful for the questions to be written down and for students to make a note of their answers): *Can you make different sounds from the same bar of the xylophone? What can you do to ensure that you always make the same sound? Are all the bars the same? What are the differences? Which bars generate high pitch? Which generate low pitch? Can you make a generalisation about the relationship between length and sound? Have we carried out a fair test?*

- Show Video P4: Playing the guitar. Discuss how sounds are produced on the guitar and, if possible, use a guitar to show how altering the length of a string (holding it against a fret) can change the pitch. The strings are all the same length so, for a fair comparison, only one string should be investigated at a time. Ensure that the students have the opportunity to feel the vibrations in the instrument by allowing them to touch it while it is being played. Ask them to observe the vibrations in the string. If the thickest string is used, they may be able to see the change in the vibrations as the string is shortened. Show them that tightening the string can also alter the pitch. Ask them to predict how the vibrations will change as the string is tightened and to observe the string to check their prediction.

Graded activities

1 Make sure each student has their own drinking straws for this activity and discourage them from blowing into each other's straws for health reasons. Let the students experiment and discuss their observations and conclusions before moving on.

2 Have the students work in groups to make a model wind instrument with bottles and water. Discuss their observations and make sure the students know that the fuller the bottle, the shorter the column of air, and therefore the higher the pitch.

3 Students can do the design part of this activity in class, but they can make their instruments at home. Remind them to bring them to class for the next lesson so they can demonstrate how they work.

Consolidate and review

- Prepare a set of sound key words on cards. Hand these out to different students and let them explain the concepts. Allow the other students to decide whether the explanation is sufficient and, if not, to suggest what information needs to be added to it.

- Let students complete their sound concept maps. Once they have done so, collect them all and hand them out at random. Let the students examine the concept map they receive and allow them to suggest additions and corrections. Let them write a comment on how easy it was for them to understand the work before collecting them again and returning them to their creators.

Differentiation

■ All of the students should be able to make the whistles and explain how the length impacts the pitch and should realise that the shortest straws produce the highest notes.

● Most of the students should be able to produce sounds and say which bottles produce the highest pitch. They should realise that when they tap the bottle below the water, the water vibrates and this creates a different sound effect. Students who can correctly label the diagrams demonstrate that they are able to organise complex concepts in a simple form.

▲ Some of the students will produce a well planned and thought out instrument with little or no help. A few students may struggle to come up with ideas. If this is the case, make a list of possible instruments (shakers, homemade drums, horns, box or tin guitars, block of wood xylophones, and so on) for them to consider.

Physics • Topic 4 Sound Consolidation

Consolidation

Student's Book page 70
Physics learning objectives

- Explore how sounds are made when objects, materials or air vibrate and learn to measure the volume of sound in decibels with a sound level meter.
- Investigate how sound travels through different materials to the ear.
- Investigate how some materials are effective in preventing sound from travelling through them.
- Investigate the way pitch describes how high or low a sound is and that high and low sounds can be loud or soft. Secondary sources can be used.
- Explore how pitch can be changed in musical instruments in a range of ways.

Resources
- Assessment Sheets P1 and P2
- Workbook page 59

Looking back

- Use the summary points to review the key things the students have learned in the topic. Prepare some close procedure sentences based on the summary points and ask the students to complete these by filling in the missing words.
- Ask students to write three sentences about new things they learned in this topic. Let them tell their group about the new things they learned and say why they found these things interesting.
- Use Workbook page 59 as an additional assessment and consolidation task to check that students have understood the main concepts in this topic.

How well do you remember?

You may use the revision and consolidation activities on Student's Book page 70 either as a test or as a paired class activity. If you are using the activities as a test, have the students work on their own to complete the tasks in writing and then collect and mark the work. If you are using them as a class activity you may prefer to let the students do some of the tasks orally (although they do need to write and draw to show how to make sounds with glass bottles). Circulate as they discuss the questions and observe the students carefully to see who is confident and who is unsure of the concepts.

Some suggested answers
1. Talking (moving their mouths), clapping hands, stamping feet, and so on.
2. a The skin of the drum.
   b The strings.
   c The air inside the instrument.
   d The strings inside the instrument.
3. By blocking your ears using earplugs or ear protectors OR by preventing the sound from travelling to your ears in the first place using soundproofing materials.
4. a It can damage your hearing; it can disturb your sleep or prevent you from concentrating; it can make you angry with your neighbours, and so on.
   b Students' own answers; any sounds above 85 to 90 decibels can damage your hearing.
5. Students own ideas, but must include some kind of vibration.

Assessment

A more formal assessment of the students' understanding of the topic can be undertaken using Assessment Sheets P1 and P2. These can be completed in class or as a homework task.

Students following Cambridge Primary Science Framework will write progression tests set and supplied by Cambridge International Examinations at this level and feedback will be given regarding their achievement levels.

Assessment Sheet answers

Assessment Sheet P1
1. a false; b true; c false [3]
2. a gas; b solid [2]
3. The pan lid; the pan; the elastic band; the air over the mouth of the bottle. [4]
4. Metres per second. [1]

Assessment Sheet P2
1. a true; b true; c false; d false [4]
2. a To protect our hearing from damage caused by loud sounds.
   b They block some of the sound. [2]
3. volume, vibration, pitch, low [4]

Physics • Topic 4 Sound Student's Book answers

Student's Book answers

pages 54–55
1. Guitar – music; referee – whistle blowing; bell – ringing; phone – ringtone or music; alarm clock – alarm ringing or music; drum – music.
2. Guitar – string, whistle – air; bell – metal; phone – speaker and air, alarm clock – speaker and air; drum – skin.
3. Students should answer yes.

pages 56–57
1. 135 decibels
2. 140 decibels
3. No, it has a volume of 70–80 decibels. However, people who mow all the time should probably protect their ears.
4. The microphone records the sound and the meter measures its volume. The sound level is displayed digitally on a small screen.
5. Suggested answers: 53.8 dB – someone talking quietly; 125.1 dB – loud fireworks or an airplane taking off.

pages 58–59
1. No, we are further away, so the sound is fainter.
2. Students should hear the tapping quite clearly.
3. Through solids.

pages 60–61
1. Students' own answers (they probably will hear sounds from outside).
2. The room is specially built so that the walls and any other openings are soundproof. Sound cannot travel into the studio through the special materials used to build it.
3. The vibrations of the drill against the ground.
4. He is wearing special ear protectors (ear muffs).
5. To make it safe for them to work by protecting their ears from noise damage, and also to make the work less unpleasant as the constant noise would be very annoying.

pages 62–63
1. The person with the wooden floors as they would hear the vibrations through the solid wood and floor space.
2. Students' answers could include curtains, carpets or rugs, thick walls, double-glazed windows, and so on.
3. Students' own ideas, but essentially they are placed in a position where they will absorb vibrations and prevent sound travelling through them.

pages 64–65
1. a recorder
   b The children are blowing the instruments.
2. The xylophone – you strike the wooden (or metal) slats to make sounds.
3. Flute, oboe, piccolo, tuba, and so on.
4. Most strings are made of metal or nylon today, but some may be made with vegetable fibres, fibres from dried animal intestines (catgut) or silk.

pages 66–67
1. Students' own suggestions. Allow them to judge whether the sounds suggested are high- or low-pitched.
2. Violin – it is the smallest instrument and has the shortest strings, so they will vibrate fastest.
3. Low – the double bass is larger and has thick, long strings that will vibrate fairly slowly.

pages 68–69
1. sounds (musical notes)
2. B – the shortest one as it will vibrate the fastest
3. The piccolo – the column of air inside it is short, so the vibrations will be fast.
4. Students' explanations should include some indication of how the musician changes the length of the column of air inside the instrument.
5. By striking different panels/keys on the instrument; the shorter panels will produce the highest-pitched notes.

Physics • Topic 5 Electricity and magnetism

5.1 Electrical circuits

Student's Book pages 72–73

Physics learning objective
- Construct complete circuits using switch, cell (battery), wire and lamps.

Resources
- Workbook pages 60 and 61
- DVD Activity P2: Electricity and safety
- Slideshow P2: Circuit components
- Slideshow P3: Batteries

Classroom equipment
- large sheets of paper
- materials for making posters

Scientific enquiry skills
- *Obtain and present evidence:* Make relevant observations and comparisons in a variety of contexts.

Key words
- **component**
- **circuit**
- **wire**
- **lamp**
- **battery (cell)**
- **switch**
- **break**

Scientific background

Students should remember some of the work on circuits that they did in Stage 2. This unit is designed to revise the basic concepts. Emphasise the need for a complete circuit from one end of the battery through the wire to the bulb and back through the second wire to the other end of the battery.

Electric current can only flow when a circuit is complete. At this level, we refer to electricity 'travelling' rather than making any reference to current flow. The students should understand that electricity travels along wires, and that we can use switches to turn lights on and off. The simple switch in the circuit goes off when we stop pressing it; most switches toggle between on and off.

A switch is a device that puts an intentional break in an electrical circuit; it can be closed when required, to control the flow of current. The switch works by creating a gap in the circuit. At low voltage, the gap only needs to be small. There are different kinds of switch in common use. Most are 'on/off' switches, which can be of two types: a push-switch, which is usually only 'on' when you press it, and a toggle or rocker switch, which stays in the position you put it. Correct terminology for 'on' is 'closed' and 'off' is 'open'.

Strictly speaking, *battery* means 'battery of cells' and refers to a number of cells in series. For instance, a 12V car battery is made from six 2V batteries. Cells are used as simple sources of electricity. When two or more cells are connected together, they form a battery.

When adding a second battery it should be placed in series with the first battery. The positive end of one battery should be against the negative end of the other. If the batteries are linked incorrectly the circuit will not work. Students should realise this from their own life experience.

Introduction

- Ask the class: *What do you remember about electrical circuits?* Let the students call out their answers and jot these down on the board as they do so. Make sure they do not repeat what others have said, and only add new information.
- Remind the class that all electricity must be treated with care, but mains electricity in particular. Use DVD Activity P2: Electricity and safety to identify and discuss potential hazards related to electricity.
- Display the term 'circuit components' and ask the class what this means. Show Slideshow P2: Circuit components and let the students identify each component and say what it does in a circuit.

Physics • Topic 5 Electricity and magnetism 5.1

Teaching and learning activities

- Turn to Student's Book page 72. Look at the circuit shown and discuss the questions orally. Let the students read through the information on the page in pairs before they answer question 4. Take their responses.
- Ask the students to complete Workbook page 60 individually. Check their answers to make sure they know the basic components, what they are for and how they are connected in a circuit.

Graded activities

1 Place the students in groups and give each group a sheet of paper to record their suggestions. Let the groups display their completed sheets of paper so they can compare theirs with others. Allow them to add any crucial information before moving on.

2 Let the students work in groups to plan and produce their posters. If possible, you could work with the Stage 2 teacher and allow your students to either present their posters to the younger students or display them in the classroom for the younger students to read and comment on.

3 Students can do this activity individually or in pairs. If students are interested in batteries and how they work, encourage them to view Slideshow P3: Batteries as an extension activity.

Consolidate and review

- Ask the students to complete Workbook page 61 and check their answers to informally assess their understanding of circuits and how they work.
- Have a class discussion around the different posters. Ask the class to develop a list of criteria for a 'good' poster and record this on the board. Then display some or all of the posters and let the students decide whether they meet the criteria or not. If not, ask them to make constructive suggestions for how the posters could be improved.
- Discuss how many different kinds of batteries the students have found. If you like, you could have a discussion about how to safely dispose of spent batteries and the value (economic and environmental) of using rechargeable batteries as much as possible.

Differentiation

■ All of the students should be able to contribute to the group discussion. They should be able to produce a comprehensive list of what you need to know before you can build an electrical circuit.

● Most of the students should be able to produce well presented, easy to understand and useful posters.

▲ Some of the students will produce comprehensive lists detailing the differences between different types of batteries.

Physics • Topic 5 Electricity and magnetism 5.2

5.2 Building circuits

Student's Book pages 74–75
Physics learning objective
- Construct complete circuits using switch, cell (battery), wire and lamps.

Resources
- Workbook pages 62–64
- Slideshow P4: Making a simple circuit
- Slideshow P5: Which will work?
- Slideshow P6: Making a circuit

Classroom equipment
- circuit components
- wire of different lengths for testing (any thin wire will do) and suitable cutter

Scientific enquiry skills
- *Obtain and present evidence:* Make relevant observations and comparisons in a variety of contexts; present results in drawings, bar charts and tables.
- *Consider evidence and approach:* Identify simple trends and patterns in results and suggest explanations for some of these; link evidence to scientific knowledge and understanding in some contexts.

Key words
- **circuit**
- **component**
- **bulb**
- **lamp**
- **switch**
- **wire**
- **connect**

⚠️ Make sure students work safely and carefully with circuit components, particularly lamps. Supervise them if they are cutting wire.

Scientific background

This unit is a practical one in which the students apply what they learned in the previous lesson and gain further experience and knowledge of circuits. Students tend to enjoy working with components to build systems. They should understand that a circuit is built up of different components. All circuits need a source of power (in this case batteries), wires and bulbs (or other items that show the effects). When the circuit is closed, the current flows and the bulb lights up because the current through the filament makes it glow.

Introduction

- Before moving on to building circuits, view Slideshow P4: Making a simple circuit with the class. Let the students explain what is happening in each step. Discuss what would happen if any wire was not connected to a component, or if the connections were not good.
- Use Slideshow P5: Which will work? to identify closed and complete circuits in which all the components are connected correctly. Let the students explain why the incomplete circuits will not work.

Teaching and learning activities

- Direct the students to Student's Book pages 74 and 75. Ask them to read through the information and answer the questions in pairs. Take feedback on the answers.
- Explain that when a circuit does not work you need to work systematically to find out what the problem could be. Make sure the students know that this is called 'troubleshooting' so that the term is not unfamiliar to them when they come to complete Activity 2.

Physics • Topic 5 Electricity and magnetism 5.2

Graded activities

1 Make sure each group has the components they need to build the circuits. If you do not have enough, you may like to do this as a student-led demonstration in which one student comes up and follows the instructions given by the class to build the circuit. The whole class then draws the completed circuit in their workbooks (Workbook page 62).

2 Remind the students that they worked with 'decision tree'-type flow diagrams when they dealt with simple keys in Topic 2. Let them work in pairs to complete the troubleshooting flow diagram on Workbook page 63 for finding problems in a circuit.

3 The students can work in pairs or small groups to develop and test the hypothesis and complete Workbook page 64. In reality, electricians try to have the shortest possible length of cable connecting parts of a circuit. This reduces the distance the current has to flow but also makes it easier to check for faults in the event of a problem. Naturally, it is cheaper and more efficient as well.

Consolidate and review

- Compare the circuits that students built in Activity 1. Look for different ways of connecting the components and ask the class: *Are they all the same? What is different between these two? Does it matter how you connect the components?* (Be aware that a buzzer must be connected in a particular direction, but other components can be placed either way round.)

- Give the students a chance to report back on the four lamp and one battery investigation (question 2 on Workbook page 62). Allow them to suggest how they could make the four lamps burn more brightly still using one battery.

- Compare the troubleshooting flow diagrams and discuss what students selected as the first item to check. Let them justify their choices. It makes sense to check that the bulb is not broken as a first choice, but they may have other ideas.

- Discuss how troubleshooting flow diagrams used by different professionals, such as electricians, air-conditioning technicians, computer programmers and so on, would be similar (but slightly more complex).

- Use Slideshow P6: Making a circuit as an extension activity. Note that students do not need to use circuit symbols at this stage. However, it is useful for them to see them as this is how circuits would be drawn in any real-life context.

Differentiation

■ All of the students should be able to join the components and build a simple circuit. If students cannot do this, you will need to spend some time working one-to-one with them to show them how to do it.

● Most of the students should be able to complete the steps shown, although some may find it difficult to know what to do after this stage. Allow them to discuss this with each other and ask them questions if necessary to help them work out that they need yes/no options. For example, if the first question is: 'Is the bulb burnt out?', the answer 'yes' would lead to the suggestion to replace the bulb; the answer 'no' would require them to check something else and to offer a yes/no option as a response.

▲ Some of the students should be able to plan an investigation using wire of different lengths. They will do a fair test with a control circuit that they can use for comparison.

Physics • Topic 5 Electricity and magnetism 5.3

5.3 Why won't it work?

Student's Book pages 76–77

Physics learning objective
- Explore how an electrical device will not work if there is a break in the circuit.

Resources
- Workbook pages 65 and 66
- Slideshow P7: Electricity
- Slideshow P8: Sources of electricity
- Slideshow P9: Circuit breakers
- Slideshow P10: Electrical devices
- Image P1: Electric flex

Classroom equipment
- flashlight with batteries removed

Scientific enquiry skills
- *Ideas and evidence:* Collect evidence in a variety of contexts; Test an idea or prediction based on scientific knowledge and understanding.
- *Plan investigative work:* Design a fair test and plan how to collect sufficient evidence.
- *Obtain and present evidence:* Make relevant observations and comparisons in a variety of contexts.
- *Consider evidence and approach:* Link evidence to scientific knowledge and understanding in some contexts.

Key words
- circuit
- break

⚠ Mains electricity is extremely dangerous. Make sure students work responsibly and safely with all electrical devices.

Scientific background

Electricity can only flow when a circuit is complete. The students should understand that electricity travels along wires, and we can use switches to break circuits and turn lights on and off. Devices cannot work if the circuit is incomplete or the switch is off. Broken or frayed wire will make a gap in a circuit, a broken or burnt out lamp will not allow current to flow through it, and fuses may break circuits in some cases.

Fuses are found in some plugs, electricity supply boards and many control panels, particularly in cars. The role of the fuse is to prevent too large a current from passing through the circuit, as this can damage devices. Fuses contain a thin wire (called fuse wire). If the current is too high, the wire heats up and melts. When the wire melts, the circuit is broken and no current can flow through the circuit.

Introduction

- Show the students Slideshow P7: Electricity and Slideshow P8: Sources of electricity to revise the basic circuit concept and to introduce the idea that some devices work when they are connected to the mains electricity supply. You may need to explain that mains electricity is a massive, complex and often unseen circuit, but that it essentially functions in the same way as the circuits they have built. The devices attached to the mains are like the lamps they observed – when the circuit is complete and closed the device will work (as long as it is not itself faulty).

- If possible, show the class a flashlight (remove the batteries). Switch it on and ask the students to suggest what the problem could be. Take suggestions and check whether they are correct. Ask what else could have caused the flashlight not to work. (If this is not possible, direct students to problem 1 on Student's Book page 76.)

- Turn to Student's Book page 76. Look at the desk lamp. Let the students suggest why it might not light up.

Physics • Topic 5   Electricity and magnetism 5.3

Teaching and learning activities

- Remind the class that a switch is used to make a gap in the circuit and stop the electricity from travelling around the circuit. The switch is a circuit breaker. Use Slideshow P9: Circuit breakers to show the class examples of switches, fuses and other objects that could cause a gap in a circuit.
- Tell the students to read silently through the information in their Student's Books and to tell each other what they read.
- Use Slideshow P10: Electrical devices. Show each device and ask the students to say what they would check first if it was not working. Let them suggest as many reasons as they can think of why the device might not work. Make sure they relate their reasons to the concept of a circuit breaker.

Graded activities

1 Let the students work in pairs to complete the activity. They should work with the same person as they did to develop their troubleshooting chart.

2 Let the students complete Workbook page 65 individually. Once they have done so, let them get together with another student to compare and discuss their answers.

3 Students should work in small groups to design and draw a testing system. They do not have to make this, but they do need to be able to explain how it works and to link their ideas back to the scientific concepts they have learned. They can record their ideas on Workbook page 66.

Consolidate and review

- Choose any of the electrical devices you have available. Tell the students it is not working and ask them to suggest what you should check to find the reason why it is not working.
- Show the class image P1: Electrical flex. Ask them to describe the flex and to explain (based on their investigation) how they would check a length of flex to make sure it was intact. Note that it would make sense to test the entire thing to start with and then to eliminate rather than to test one by one.

Differentiation

■ All of the students should be able to suggest at least the most obvious things to check, based on their life experiences. More able students will think more critically and list the problems from most to least likely.

● Most of the students should be able to make at least one suggestion, although some may have difficulty eliminating the items already tested.

▲ The quality of responses and suggestions will depend on how well the students understand the concept of a circuit and a circuit breaker. Some of the students should realise that if the wire is fine, it will work in a circuit and make a lamp light up. More able students will test the whole thing and then eliminate options.

Physics • Topic 5 Electricity and magnetism 5.4

5.4 Electrical current

Student's Book pages 78–79

Physics learning objective
- Know that electrical current flows and that models can describe this flow, e.g. particles travelling around a circuit.

Resources
- Workbook pages 67 and 68
- Slideshow P11: Power stations
- Slideshow P12: Electricity generation

Classroom equipment
- for demonstration: metre rule and glass marbles

Scientific enquiry skills
- *Obtain and present evidence:* Make relevant observations and comparisons in a variety of contexts.

Key words
- flow
- current
- particles

⚠️ Mains electricity is dangerous. Remind students of the safely rules and make sure they know not to touch overhead cables or climb pylons as this will be lethal.

Scientific background

Electricity results from the movement of tiny particles called *electrons,* which carry an *electric charge,* and the flow of these charged particles is called an *electric current.* Power stations or batteries 'push' electric current along wires. We attach electrical devices to the electric current by plugging them into a *mains socket* or by putting batteries inside them. The electric current provides the *energy* to make the device work.

Students have not yet studied particle models so they do not know about atoms and electrons; also, the concept of electrical current is very abstract and difficult, so it is adequate to use models of flow to describe it at this level. It is not correct to describe this flow as similar to water through a pipe, but it is useful to model it by lining up glass marbles against a metre rule. The marbles should be close but not touching. Give the end marble a sharp push and you will see that most of the marbles in the row move only a little distance, while the one on the other end shoots off quite quickly. This is a more scientifically accurate model of electron movement and it shows how quickly the current flows through the marbles.

Introduction

- Show the class the images of power stations using Slideshow P11: Power stations. Ask: *What happens at a power station? Are power stations right next to the places that use the electricity?* (not usually) *Can you explain the way electricity gets from the power station to our homes?*

- Use Slideshow P12: Electricity generation to introduce the idea that electricity is generated at a source and then pumped (use the analogy of a pump as this is scientifically more accurate than other terms) along wires to the places in which it is used. Ask the class: *When do we know that electricity is moving through a circuit? Can we see it?*

Teaching and learning activities

- Turn to Student's Book page 78. Remind the class that we cannot see electricity but that we can tell when it is there because it makes devices work. Discuss the questions about the fan, making sure the students can tell that the fan is working because electricity is flowing around a circuit without breaks.

- Use the diagrams and information on the Student's Book pages to explain that we can think of electricity flowing around a circuit. Use the metre rule and marbles to show the students that energy (provided by your push) can move very quickly from particle to particle (the marbles).

- Discuss the circuit diagram using phrases such as: *the battery pumps out tiny particles here* (the negative end) *and these flow around the circuit like this* (tracing the path) *back to the battery here* (the positive end) *and out again in a continuous loop.*

Physics • Topic 5 Electricity and magnetism 5.4

Graded activities

1 Ask the students to turn to Workbook page 67. Let them write down answers to the questions individually then direct them all to the flashlight. Explain that circuits in real life do not follow the format we have used to build them. Let the students trace the circuit in the diagram using their fingers, and let them check that the person next to them can find it. Then let them complete the activity on their own.

2 This is a fun group activity in which the students have to consider that the parts of the circuit do not actually move when current flows around them. They will need to take that into account when they prepare their role plays.

3 Birds can sit on single cables because the current passes through the cable and not through the birds. If they touch two wires, they short the circuit and are often killed in the process. If the bird is big enough it can cause a power outage. This is why electric cables in flight paths often have things on them to make them visible to birds. Electricians use special harnesses (among other safely equipment) to redirect the current around their bodies so they can work on cables. They still have to be careful not to cause a short. Students can formulate questions and type these into search engines to find this information quickly and easily on the internet.

Consolidate and review

- Let the different groups (some or all) show the class their role plays. Ask them to explain how and why they decided to portray current in the way they have chosen.
- Use Workbook page 68 as an informal assessment task to make sure the students recognise and can define the key vocabulary related to electricity at this level.

Differentiation

■ All of the students should be able to answer the questions and at least draw arrows to show the flow of the current. More able students will add clear labels to explain what a current is.

● You will need to observe students as they work to make sure they are all contributing and taking part. Listen carefully to their explanations to make sure they understand the general idea of electrical current.

▲ Some of the students will give clear, detailed explanations with examples and diagrams/illustrations. They will be able to provide clear answers and should be able to find some information with little or no help.

Physics • Topic 5 Electricity and magnetism 5.5

5.5 Magnets

Student's Book pages 80–81

Physics learning objective
- Explore the forces between magnets and know that magnets can attract or repel each other.

Resources
- Workbook page 69
- Slideshow P13: Uses of magnets
- Slideshow P14: Magnetic poles
- PCM P1: Magnet strength
- PCM P2: Testing magnets

Classroom equipment
- examples of different magnets
- bar magnet with poles marked for use in class
- if possible, an unpainted magnet and a piece of metal (or two metal spheres)

Scientific enquiry skills
- *Ideas and evidence:* Collect evidence in a variety of contexts.
- *Plan investigative work:* Suggest questions that can be tested and make predictions; communicate these; design a fair test and plan how to collect sufficient evidence; choose apparatus and decide what to measure.
- *Obtain and present evidence:* Begin to think about the need for repeated measurements of, for example, length.

Key words
- magnet
- pole
- force

> ⚠ If students are handling magnets, remind them not to drop them as this damages them and can change the polarity. Also remind students to keep magnets away from electronic equipment.

Scientific background

Magnets attract magnetic objects. Magnets have two poles termed north (or north-seeking) and south (or south-seeking). The Earth behaves as a giant magnet because it has an iron core.

When two magnets are put together, the opposite poles are attracted to one another, so N and S poles or S and N poles attract each other. When like poles of a magnet (N and N or S and S) are put together they repel each other, each pushing the other away. Some magnets are stronger than others but the strongest parts of any magnet are the ends, where the force field is concentrated. Only magnetic materials are affected by magnetism. The only common magnetic materials are iron and steel. The correct term for the magnetic effect is a 'field'. The field acts upon a magnetic material to create a force. For a bar magnet, the field is most concentrated at the ends (poles). A horseshoe magnet is effectively a bar magnet that has been bent into a curve. This brings the poles together and produces a stronger magnetic field.

Introduction

- Have a class discussion to find out what the students already know about magnets. Ask them to tell you how they know these things. You may also like to compile a list of questions about magnets for consideration as you work through the topic.

- Show the class Slideshow P13: Uses of magnets. As each slide is displayed, ask students to say where the magnet is, what the magnet is being used for and how it is working. Discuss whether students have seen magnets in use like this and let them share other places where they have seen or used magnets.

Physics • Topic 5   Electricity and magnetism 5.5

Teaching and learning activities

- Turn to Student's Book page 80. Look at the photographs and let the students answer questions 1 to 3 in small groups.
- Show the class a selection of differently shaped magnets (if this is not possible, you can use photographs). Point out the bar shapes, U-shapes (horseshoe shapes) and others. Point out to the students that the bar magnet has two ends, as does the U-shaped magnet. Tell them that these are called poles.
- Show the class an unpainted magnet (if you can) and a piece of metal. (Two metal spheres would work well.) Ask: *Which one is the magnet? What could you do to find out?*

Graded activities

1 Let the students work on their own to design and make a poster. Encourage them to think about uses other than the ones that they have seen in the slideshow and in their books.

2 Let the students work in pairs to answer the questions on Workbook page 69 and record their ideas. They do not have to do the test, but if they are interested and you have time, you may like to let them experiment to check their predictions.

3 Let the students do this research as a homework task. They can use reference books, CD-ROMs and/or internet sources to find the information.

Consolidate and review

- Display the completed posters in the classroom and ask the students to select their top three, giving reasons why they think these three are best.
- Depending on your resources and how much time you have, you may like to arrange the class in groups and let them do some experiments with magnets. Copy PCMs P1 and P2 and distribute these so half the groups do one task and half do the other.
  - In groups get the students to investigate how far a magnetic field can reach.
  - Give the students at least two magnets of different strengths. Tell them to place a magnet onto the '0' end of the first ruled bar on PCM 1. Tell them to place a paper clip at the 10 cm mark on the ruled bar. The students should carefully move the paper clip up the ruler towards the magnet. They should try to find out how close they have to push the paper clip to the magnet before the magnetic force pulls it onto the magnet. Mark the farthest point and record the distance from the magnet.
  - Repeat this process with a different magnet, using the second ruled bar. If there is time, use the remaining ruled bars to repeat the whole experiment with a different sized paper clip, or some other small magnetic item. Which magnet is the strongest?
  - Spend some time taking feedback and discussing results.
- Display Slideshow P14: Magnetic poles and ask the students to explain what this image means in terms of magnets and what they have discovered about them so far.

Differentiation

All of the students should be able to list at least five uses of magnets. More able students will be able to find more. They will find unusual and interesting applications and may include electromagnets.

Most of the students should be able to suggest methods of testing, including picking up the same mass with different ends of the magnet. More able students will refine their testing by using similar objects and also repeating the test for more accurate results.

Some of the students should be able to find out that the north pole of a magnet will swing to face north when the magnet is allowed to hang freely. This is because of the Earth's magnetic field and the magnetic north and south poles. More able students will explain this clearly, with diagrams.

81

Physics • Topic 5 Electricity and magnetism 5.6

5.6 Investigate magnetic forces

Student's Book pages 82–83

Physics learning objective
- Explore the forces between magnets and know that magnets can attract or repel each other.

Resources
- Workbook pages 70 and 71

Classroom equipment
- bar magnets
- iron filings and a sheet of paper
- steel pin or staple
- string or thread

Scientific enquiry skills
- *Ideas and evidence:* Collect evidence in a variety of contexts; test an idea or prediction based on scientific knowledge and understanding.

Key words
- force
- attract
- push
- pull
- repel

⚠️ Remind the students not to drop the magnets as this can damage them.

Scientific background

Magnetism and its effects are best explored by experimenting with magnets. You will find that most adults know about magnets and how they work because they have played (experimented) with them and they remember their experiences. Exploring how magnets behave allows the students to develop their own understanding of physical processes and also encourages them to draw conclusions and think deductively. This experiment will allow them to see that opposite poles attract and that like poles repel each other.

Introduction

- Remind the students that pushing and pulling are examples of forces. Let them suggest examples of both pushing and pulling forces. Ask whether they think magnets exert a pushing force or a pulling force and take answers from different students. Encourage them to justify their answers by providing evidence for their statements.

- Explain that magnets exert a magnetic force. You cannot see this force but you can use iron filings and a sheet of paper to demonstrate the force lines. Magnetic force is a non-contact force that can be felt at a distance. You can demonstrate this by placing a steel pin or staple close to a magnet and showing the students how it 'jumps' towards the magnet. Make sure they realise that the item is pulled by the magnetic force and that it does not move on its own.

Teaching and learning activities

- Tell the students that magnets exert force on other magnets. Ask them what type of force they think this will be (pushing or pulling) and how they could observe the forces between magnets. Take some ideas before asking the students to turn to Student's Book page 82. Look at the photograph and let the students explain what they think is happening.

- Ask the students to study the magnet diagram on Student's Book page 83 and let them answer questions 2 and 3 orally in groups. Tell them that they are going to do their own investigation to see what happens when magnets are placed pole to pole.

Physics • **Topic 5** **Electricity and magnetism 5.6**

Graded activities

1 Give each pair the equipment they need. Direct them to Workbook page 70. Let them read and follow the instructions independently to do the experiment and record their observations and conclusions.

2 Give the students some time to think about this and allow them to use magnets and other objects to try out and model their ideas. Allow some time in the classroom for the students to share their ideas. If time allows, you may like to allow groups to make their toys and demonstrate how they work.

3 Students can discuss this problem in groups, but they may need to do some research to answer the question. Those students who have realised that the north pole will seek north will use compass directions together with a magnet to solve the problem. Once they can get the magnet to point north (by allowing it to move freely) they can locate north and its opposite, south.

Consolidate and review

- Ask the students to summarise what they have learned about magnets so far in this topic. Check their work to make sure their points are correct.
- Use Workbook page 71 to consolidate the idea that like poles repel and unlike poles attract. Share the answers and let the students correct their own work.

Differentiation

■ All of the students should be able to read and correctly follow the instructions. Observe the students as they work and assist any who seem unsure of what to do. More able students will be able to draw accurate and clear conclusions based on their observations.

● Not all students will be able to do this activity as some will not apply what they know about forces of repulsion to the problem. You may need to show them some magnetic games, such as the floating circle magnets, to demonstrate how a magnet can appear to float in the air.

▲ Some of the students will be able to make some suggestions for doing this. They will present a series of clear steps for doing this and will be able to explain the reason for each step.

Physics • Topic 5 Electricity and magnetism 5.7

5.7 Magnets and metals

Student's Book pages 84–85

Physics learning objective
- Know that magnets attract some metals but not others.

Resources
- Workbook pages 72 and 73
- Slideshow P15: Made from metal
- Video P5: Electromagnets

Classroom equipment
- magnets
- some metal items for testing and some non-magnetic items (including aluminium foil)
- set of local coins for each group

Scientific enquiry skills
- *Ideas and evidence:* Collect evidence in a variety of contexts; test an idea or prediction based on scientific knowledge and understanding.
- *Plan investigative work:* Suggest questions that can be tested and make predictions; communicate these; design a fair test and plan how to collect sufficient evidence; choose apparatus and decide what to measure.
- *Obtain and present evidence:* Make relevant observations in a variety of contexts; present results in drawing, bar charts and tables.
- *Consider evidence and approach:* Identify simple trends and patterns in results and suggest explanations for some of these; explain what the evidence shows and whether it supports predictions. Communicate this clearly to others; link evidence to scientific knowledge and understanding in some contexts.

Key words
- **metal**
- **magnetic**
- **non-magnetic**

⚠ Make sure students do not touch sharp pieces of metal and remind them to handle magnets with care. If they are testing whether household objects (such as metal lamps) are magnetic, they should place a sheet of paper between the magnet and surface to prevent scratching it.

Scientific background

A magnet is usually made from a substance that contains iron. A magnet attracts other magnetic materials. Lodestone is a naturally occurring magnet. Materials that are attracted to magnets include metals such as iron, steel, nickel and cobalt. Not all metals are magnetic. Non-magnetic materials include plastic, wood and glass.

Magnetism can be used for making toys, for sorting materials (aluminium recycling centres), for fridge magnets and for picking-up tools. Magnets are used as components in motors and generators. The large magnets used to pick up scrap metal or heavy metal equipment are electromagnets – essentially these are magnets powered by electricity, so they are much stronger than ordinary magnets.

Introduction

- Ask the students whether magnets stick to any surface. Take some responses. Ask: *What do magnets stick to?* Show them some of the materials you have brought to class. Ask: *Will a magnet attract this?* Group the items into 'yes' and 'no' groups according to the students' answers, but do not test them or argue with the students at this stage.

- Use a magnet to check whether the predictions were correct. Take each item in turn and see whether the magnet attracts it. Introduce the terms 'magnetic' and 'non-magnetic' with reference to the two groups of materials.

Physics • Topic 5 Electricity and magnetism 5.7

- Ask the students: *What do you notice about all the materials in the magnetic group?* They should notice that they are all metal (or a combination of metal and another material). Explain that non-metals are non-magnetic (for most everyday purposes) and that some metals are also non-magnetic. Show Slideshow P15: Made from metal.

Teaching and learning activities

- Turn to Student's Book page 84. Look at the materials and let the students predict which will be non-magnetic. They should find this easy based on your introduction.

- Discuss questions 2 and 3 on Student's Book pages 84 and 85 with the class. Demonstrate that aluminium foil is non-magnetic by trying to pick it up with a magnet before asking students to answer question 3. You may also need to demonstrate that the magnets still attract each other through the foil. When you discuss question 4, reiterate that the students should never put small magnets, particularly the Buckyball (Neodymium) magnets, in their mouths.

Graded activities

1 Arrange the students in groups of four. Direct them to Workbook page 72 and let them plan, record and carry out their tests. Have a class feedback session to discuss what they discovered.

2 Students can work in the same groups of four to carry out the coin investigation. Make sure they record their predictions on Workbook page 73 before they start their investigation. If students cannot photograph the coins, show them how to do a coin rubbing to get a good image.

3 Students will have to ask adults or do their own research to find the information. You can set this activity as a homework task. Make sure they realise that they should not use a magnet to see what happens! Note that CD-ROMs are optical disks and as such are not affected by magnets.

Consolidate and review

- Use the results from Activity 1 to develop a class table of magnetic and non-magnetic metals.

- Show the class Video P5: Electromagnets. Tell them to take notes and jot down questions as they watch. Share their observations and questions and let them try to answer each other's questions. If they ask question to which you do not know the answer, tell them so and ask them how they could find the answers themselves. Make sure they realise that the magnets in the video do not exert any magnetic force until they are 'switched on'; that is why the large pieces of metal are not pulled towards the magnets, because they are positioned above them. Watch again to show this if necessary.

Differentiation

■ All of the students should have no difficulty with the investigation, but you may need to help some students identify and name metals.

● Most of the students should be able to carry out a fair test and some students will investigate further to find out what coins are made from. Students may make predictions based on the colour of coins (assuming that brown coins are made of copper and silver ones are made of steel). This is a fair assumption at this level.

▲ Some of the students will be able to explain that the magnetic force wipes the card and that all data stored on it will be lost.

Physics • Topic 5 Electricity and magnetism 5.8

5.8 Using magnets to sort metals

Student's Book pages 86–87
Physics learning objective
- Know that magnets attract some metals but not others.

Resources
- Workbook pages 74 and 75
- Slideshow P16: Recycling cans
- PCM P3: Recycling aluminium

Classroom equipment
- samples of aluminium and steel cans

Scientific enquiry skills
- *Ideas and evidence:* Collect evidence in a variety of contexts.
- *Obtain and present evidence:* Make relevant observations in a variety of contexts; present results in drawings, bar charts and tables.
- *Consider evidence and approach:* Link evidence to scientific knowledge and understanding in some contexts.

Key words
- magnetic
- non-magnetic
- aluminium
- recycle
- recycling

Scientific background

Magnetism can be very useful. It can be used for sorting magnetic objects from non-magnetic objects at recycling centres. To recycle metal cans, a magnet is used to separate the magnetic cans (made of iron and steel) from the non-magnetic aluminium cans. Iron and steel can then be recycled separately from the aluminium.

Introduction

- Write the word 'recycling' on the board. Ask the students what it means and whether they think metals can be recycled (most can be). If they say yes, ask them how they think this happens. For example, ask: *Can cars be recycled? Explain how. Can gold be recycled? Explain how. Can drink cans be recycled? Explain how,* and so on.
- Spend some time discussing why it is environmentally sound to recycle metals.

Teaching and learning activities

- Show the class an example of a steel food can (it can be unopened) and an aluminium drinks can. Use a magnet to show that the steel can is attracted by a magnet but the aluminium one is not.
- Ask the students to work in pairs to read through Student's Book pages 86 and 87, answering the questions orally as they do so.
- Once they have done this, show the class Slideshow P16: Recycling cans. Let them make comments or ask questions before moving on.

Graded activities

1 Let the students work in pairs to complete the task. Allow them to refer to the Student's Book if they need to, although the process shown on Workbook page 74 is a simplified one.

2 Let the students work in groups to discuss the activity. Give each group a copy of PCM P3: Recycling aluminium to use as a reference as they plan their posters. They can plan collaboratively but each student should draw his or her own poster using Workbook page 75.

3 You can do this activity orally as a class. Give students time to discuss the problem and share their ideas before you have a class discussion.

Physics • Topic 5 Electricity and magnetism 5.8

Consolidate and review

- Ask the students to prepare a short talk about recycling aluminium. Give some students a chance to present their talk to the class.
- Ask students to make a set of true and false statements about metals and magnetism. They should write these on cards so you can collect them. You can either hand these out at random and have students sort them into two groups (true and false) or you can ask students to come up, read a statement and say whether it is true or false and how they know this.
- Ask students to display the posters they completed for Activity 2 on their desks. Allow the students to walk around, look at each other's posters and select the three they think are the most effective. Let some students share their choices and why they think these posters are effective.

Differentiation

■ All of the students should be able to manage this task. They will give very clear and detailed labels showing that they have a good understanding of the steps in the process and why each one is important.

● Most of the students will be able to provide the basic steps. More able students will produce attractive, clear and very informative posters.

▲ Observe students as they discuss this problem in groups to see which students apply their scientific knowledge to this new context. Make sure you encourage less confident students to contribute to the class discussion by asking them questions such as: *Do you agree with what he/she has said? Can you tell me why?*

Physics • Topic 5 Electricity and magnetism Consolidation

Consolidation

Student's Book page 88

Physics learning objectives
- Construct complete circuits using switch, cell (battery) wire and lamps.
- Explore how an electrical device will not work if there is a break in the circuit.
- Know that electrical current flows and that models can describe this flow, e.g. particles travelling around a circuit.
- Explore the forces between magnets and know that magnets can attract or repel each other.
- Know that magnets attract some metals but not others.

Resources
- Assessment sheets P3, P4 and P5
- Workbook page 76

Looking back

- Use the summary points to review the key things that the students have learned in the topic. Make up some true and false statements based on the summary points. Let the students decide whether the statements are true or false.
- Ask students to complete the concept maps on Workbook page 76. Allow them to show their maps to a partner and discuss any differences.
- Ask the students to make up five questions based on what they have learned. Collect these and hand them out randomly to other students. Let them answer each other's questions.

How well do you remember?

You may use the revision and consolidation activities on Student's Book page 88 either as a test or as a paired class activity. If you are using the activities as a test, have the students work on their own to complete the tasks in writing and then collect and mark the work. If you are using them as a class activity, you may prefer to let the students do the tasks orally (although they do need to draw the circuits in question 1). Circulate as they discuss the questions and observe them carefully to see who is confident and who is unsure of the concepts.

Some suggested answers

1. Students' own circuits.
2. Check that it is plugged in and that the plug is switched on at the wall; check that the power is not out; check that the on/off switch is working; check that the cord is not frayed or broken anywhere along its length.
3. Only by observing its effect, in other words, the lamp is lit or the device is working.
4. The magnets will push each other away/repel each other.
5. Not if the magnet is strong enough to exert a force through it.
6. aluminium, gold, silver, copper, zinc, stainless steel
7. Run the magnet over the material several times to remove the steel from the aluminium.

Assessment

A more formal assessment of the students' understanding of the topic can be undertaken using Assessment Sheets P3, P4 and P5. These can be completed in class or as a homework task.

Students following Cambridge Primary Science Framework will write progression tests set and supplied by Cambridge International Examinations at this level and feedback will be given regarding their achievement levels.

Assessment Sheet answers

Assessment Sheet P3
1. Check students' diagrams. [5]
2. a false; b false [2]
3. more, energy, broken [3]

Assessment Sheet P4
1. A switch is used…to stop the electricity flowing in a circuit.
   Electrical current…flows around a circuit in a continuous loop.
   A circuit is a closed path which…allows electricity to flow around it. [3]
2. wires, flow, particles, electrons [4]
3. B [1]
4. a false; b true [2]

Assessment Sheet P5
1. Check students' diagrams. [3]
2. separate, recycled [2]
3. iron, steel [2]
4. a true; b false; c false [3]

Physics • Topic 5 Electricity and magnetism Student's Book answers

Student's Book answers

pages 72–73
1. Two lamps, wire, a battery and a switch.
2. No, the switch is open.
3. Close the switch to complete the circuit.
4. Flat battery, burnt-out lamp, faulty or loose connections on the wires.

pages 74–75
1. Students' own explanations.
2. Students' suggestions could include: check that the battery is the right way round in the holder; check that the lamp is not broken; check that the battery is not flat.

pages 76–77
1. Students' suggestions could include: for flashlight – flat battery, broken bulb, switch not making contact; for lamp – burnt-out bulb, not plugged in, power outage and similar.
2. Devices are plugged into the mains at the wall and the mains switch has to be on for the current to flow. The device also has its own on/off switch to allow the current to flow to it.

pages 78–79
1. The blades will turn and the fan will work.
2. From the mains supply, via the wall plug.
3. It is transmitted via electrical cables to the home and then through circuits in the wall to the device itself.
4. Students' own explanations – check that they use the words 'current', 'flow' and 'particles'.

pages 80–81
1. Students' own answers based on their experiences.
2. Students' own answers based on their experiences.
3. The size, thickness and shape of the magnet as well as the materials used to make it will affect its strength. Magnets can lose their magnetism if they are left stuck to metal objects for a long time or if they are stored carelessly and/or dropped.
4. You can test it by placing it against something made of steel or iron to see if it sticks.

pages 82–83
1. Two of the magnets are stuck together but the other two are pushing each other away.
2. It suggests that magnets can exert both pushing and pulling forces and that they can attract each other (stick together) or repel each other (push each other apart).
3. They would stick together as the opposite poles would still be facing each other.

pages 84–85
1. Students' own ideas, but at the very least they should suggest all of the materials besides the metals.
2. The magnet exerts a force and the material is attracted by the magnet.
3. The magnets would still stick together because aluminium foil is non-magnetic.
4. There have been reported cases where children have swallowed a few magnets and these have resulted in injury and at least one reported death. Swallowing small powerful magnets can result in intestinal injury requiring surgery. The magnets attract each other through the walls of the stomach and intestine, perforating the bowel. The Centres for Disease Control in the USA reported 33 cases requiring surgery and one death during 2009. The magnets had been swallowed by young children (accidently) and teens (who were using two magnets to pretend to have tongue piercings).

pages 86–87
1. You can run a magnet over the scraps; any pins will stick to the magnet and you can remove them. Once you have cleared a section, you can remove the fabric and do the next section.
2. From a variety of sources: people collect them on the street and take them to recycling centres where they are paid by the kilogram for the scrap; households recycle cans; local waste removal services may have recycling policies in place and will separate cans from other waste.
3. To ensure that no steel cans manage to pass through the system – if they pass through one magnetic head, they will be caught by the second one.

PCM B1: Model arm muscle

Follow the instructions to make a model arm muscle.

1 Fold a piece of paper in half.

2 Cut across the fold vertically.

3 Open the paper out and glue the edge. Bend to make a tube and stick the edges together.

4 When the 'muscle' is relaxed it is long and thin.

5 When the 'muscle' is contracted it is short and fat.

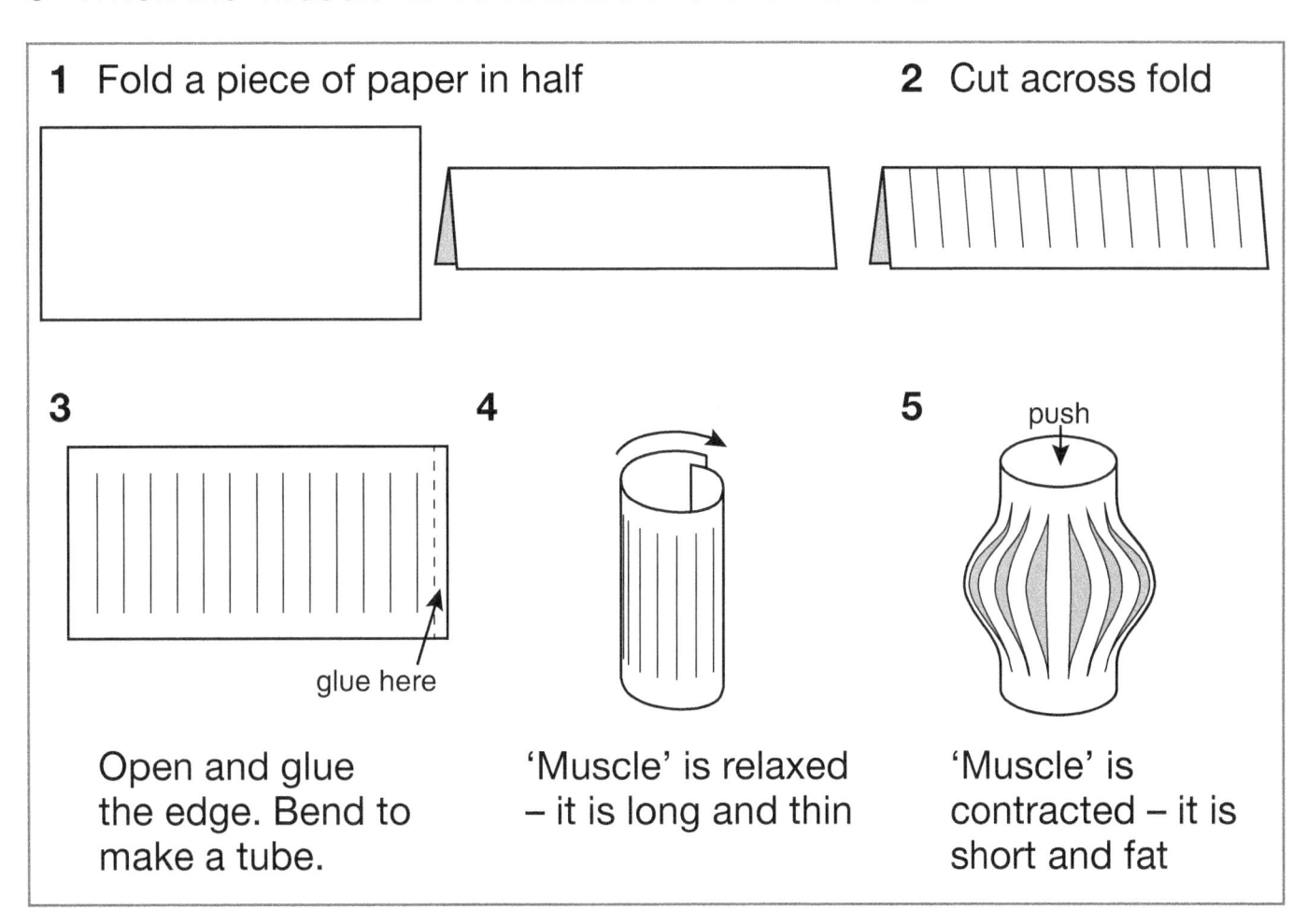

1 Fold a piece of paper in half

2 Cut across fold

3 Open and glue the edge. Bend to make a tube.

4 'Muscle' is relaxed – it is long and thin

5 'Muscle' is contracted – it is short and fat

1.10 Different medicines

PCM B2: Aloe vera

Aloe vera is a plant with thick, fleshy leaves. It is grown commercially for use in herbal medicines and cosmetics. Many people believe that it has healing and soothing properties.

The ancient Egyptians believed that Aloe vera was the 'plant of immortality'. This means that they believed it helped you to stay young.

There is very little scientific evidence that Aloe vera has any medicinal properties, although many people believe that it does.

Scientists know that Aloe vera contains natural chemicals which can kill some types of bacteria and germs.

Aloe vera creams are safe to use and some people say that they soothe sunburn and other skin conditions.

Some people drink Aloe vera juice to help with digestion. If the juice is too strong it can cause side effects, such as diarrhoea.

Tissues and wet wipes often contain Aloe vera because of its moisturising effect.

Aloe vera is safe to use but scientists argue that it does not work as a medicine

1.10 Different medicines

PCM B3: Medicines wordsearch

1. Write down ten words that have something to do with drugs and medicines.

   _____ _____ _____ _____ _____

   _____ _____ _____ _____ _____

2. Use these words to make a wordsearch puzzle.
   Write them on the grid. Words can go vertically, horizontally or diagonally.
   Fill the empty blocks with letters.

3. Exchange puzzles with a partner. Try to find each other's words.

2.2 Adapting to different habitats

PCM B4: Poar bear coats

You will need:
- three containers, each containing cotton wool soaked in warm water
- large container of icy water
- choice of fabrics to represent the polar bear 'coat' (e.g wool, cotton wool, leather, fleece, linen)
- thermometer

Follow the instructions below to carry out your experiment.

1 Wrap each of your containers in different fabric.

2 Place the containers in the icy water.

3 Put a piece of warm cotton wool into each container.

4 Measure the temperature of the cotton wool at regular intervals and record the results in your Workbook, pages 16–18. Remember to keep the end (bulb) of the thermometer in the cotton wool and to read the scale at eye level.

Think about it!

What can you do to make this a fair test?

2.4 Identifying and grouping animals

PCM B5: Similarities and differences in birds

In what ways are these birds the same? In what ways are they different?

Stage 4 Collins Primary Science 2014   95

2.5 Using identification keys

PCM B6: Small animal card sort

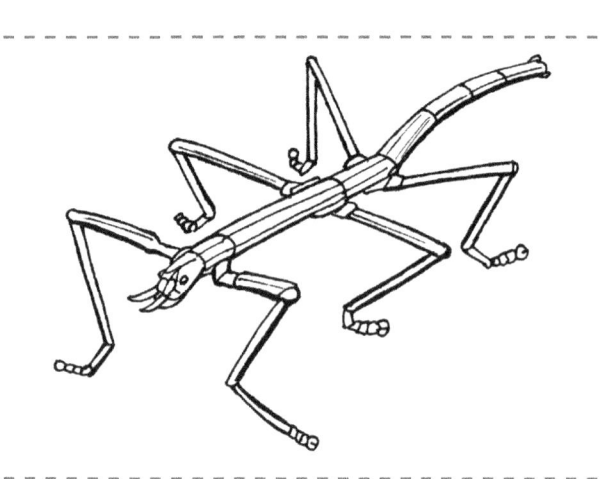

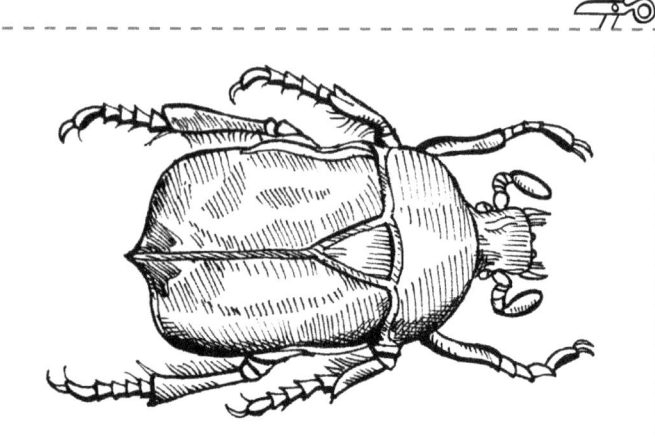

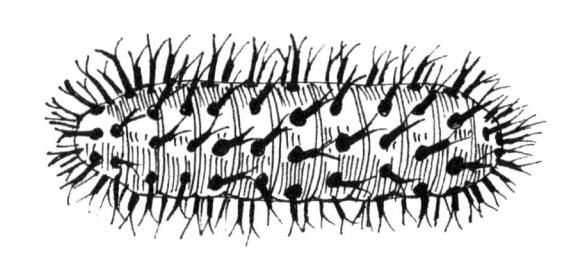

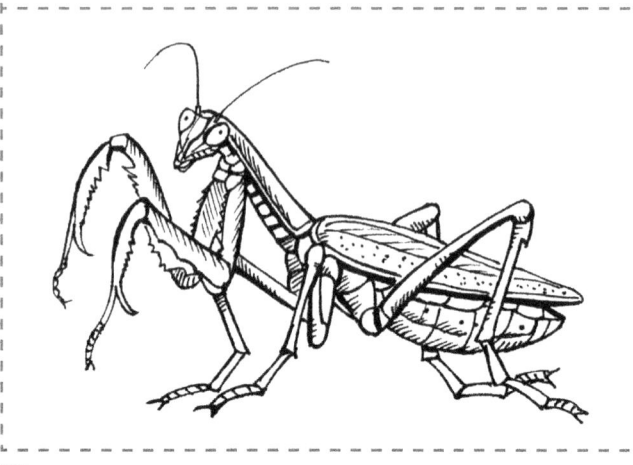

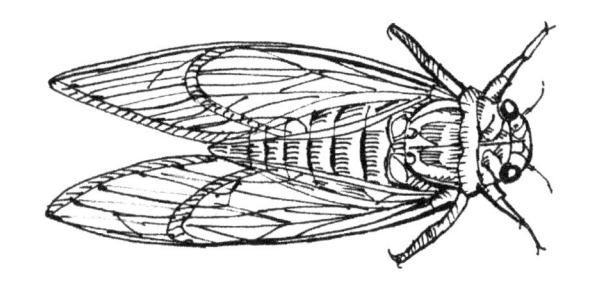

96 Stage 4 Collins Primary Science 2014

Topic 2 Looking back

PCM B7: Identifying wild cats

Petra has made this key to identify the five types of wild cat she saw at the zoo. The cats are: lion, black panther, tiger, leopard and cheetah. Use it to help answer the questions on page 38 of the Student's Book.

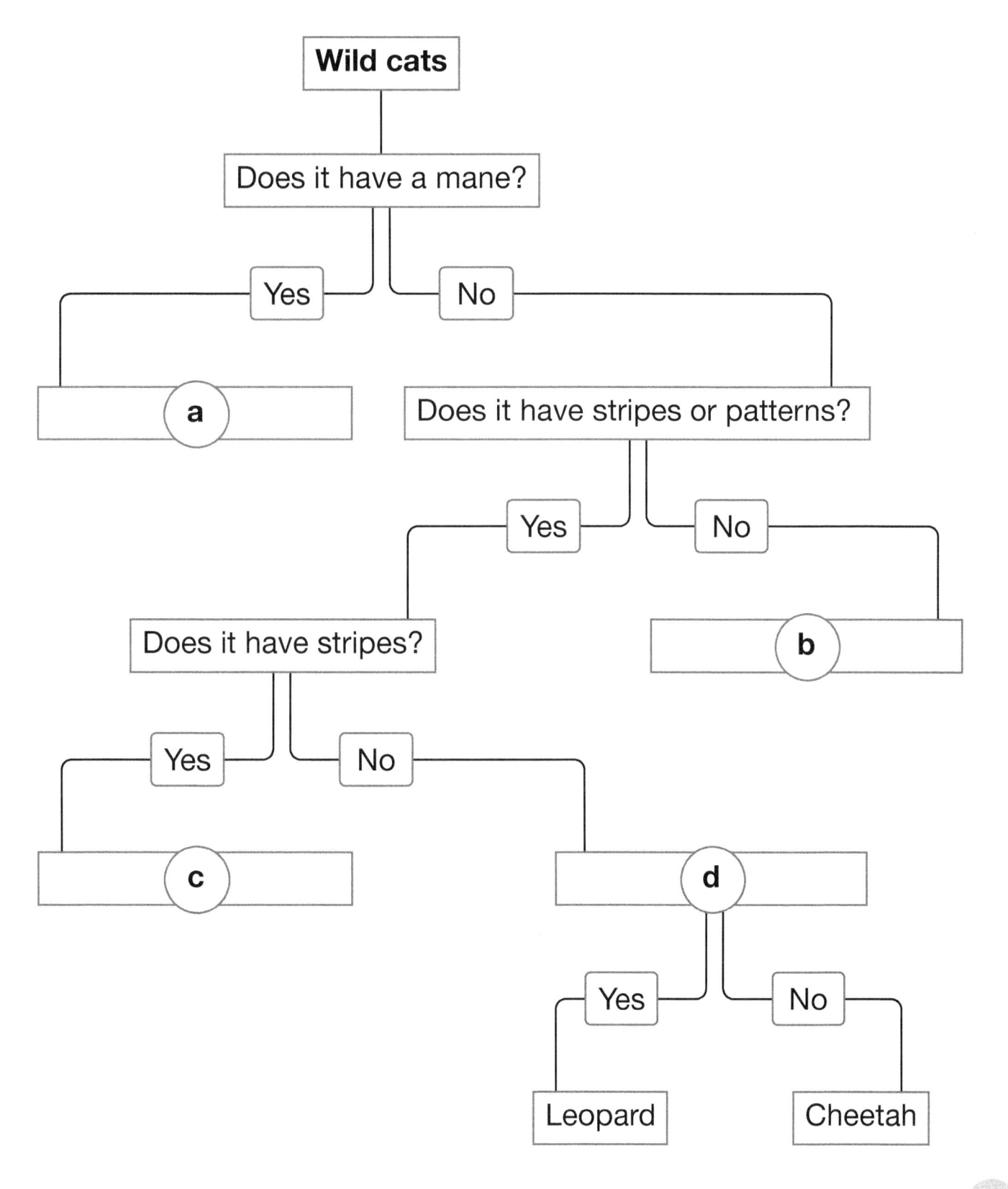

```
                        Wild cats
                           |
                  Does it have a mane?
                     /            \
                   Yes             No
                   /                 \
                 [ a ]        Does it have stripes or patterns?
                                   /            \
                                 Yes             No
                                 /                 \
                        Does it have stripes?     [ b ]
                           /         \
                         Yes          No
                         /              \
                       [ c ]            [ d ]
                                        /    \
                                      Yes     No
                                      /        \
                                  Leopard    Cheetah
```

Stage 4 Collins Primary Science 2014   97

3.6 Gas to liquid

PCM C1: Condensation

_____

_____

_____

_____

_____

_____

_____

_____

_____

_____

PCM P1: Magnet strength

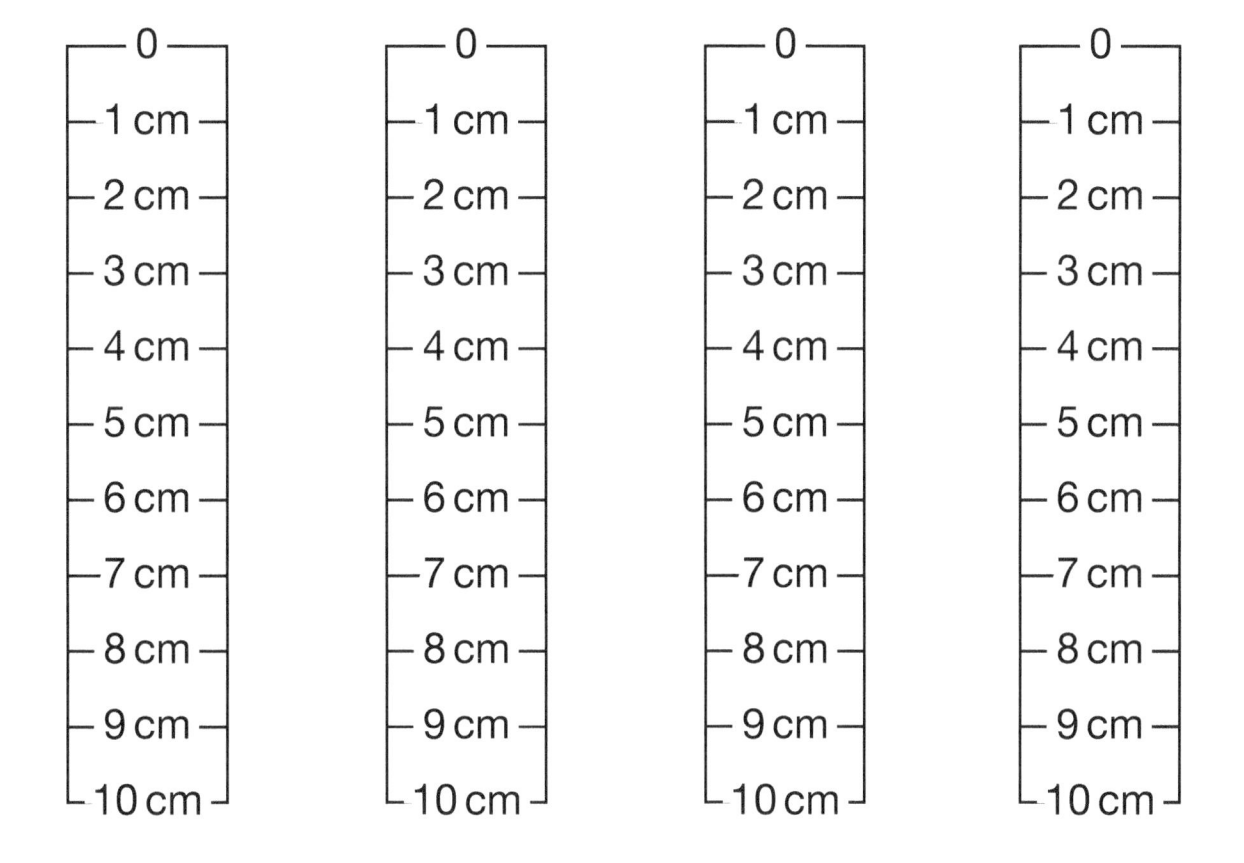

0	0	0	0
1 cm	1 cm	1 cm	1 cm
2 cm	2 cm	2 cm	2 cm
3 cm	3 cm	3 cm	3 cm
4 cm	4 cm	4 cm	4 cm
5 cm	5 cm	5 cm	5 cm
6 cm	6 cm	6 cm	6 cm
7 cm	7 cm	7 cm	7 cm
8 cm	8 cm	8 cm	8 cm
9 cm	9 cm	9 cm	9 cm
10 cm	10 cm	10 cm	10 cm

5.5 Magnets

PCM P2: Testing magnets

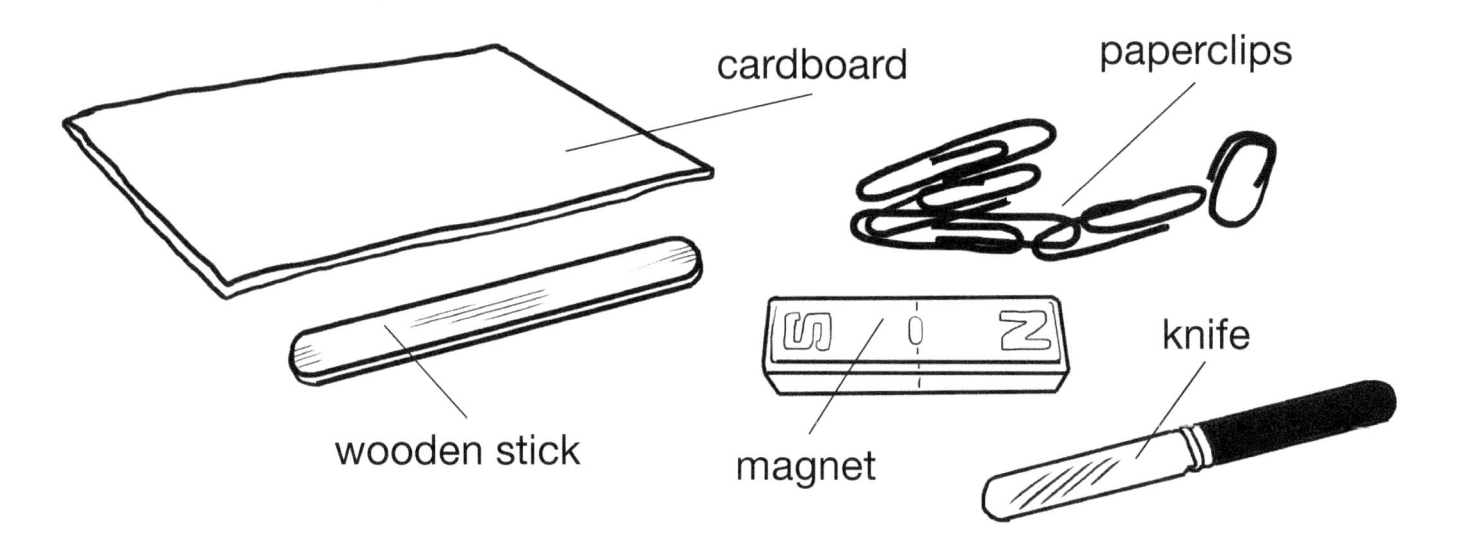

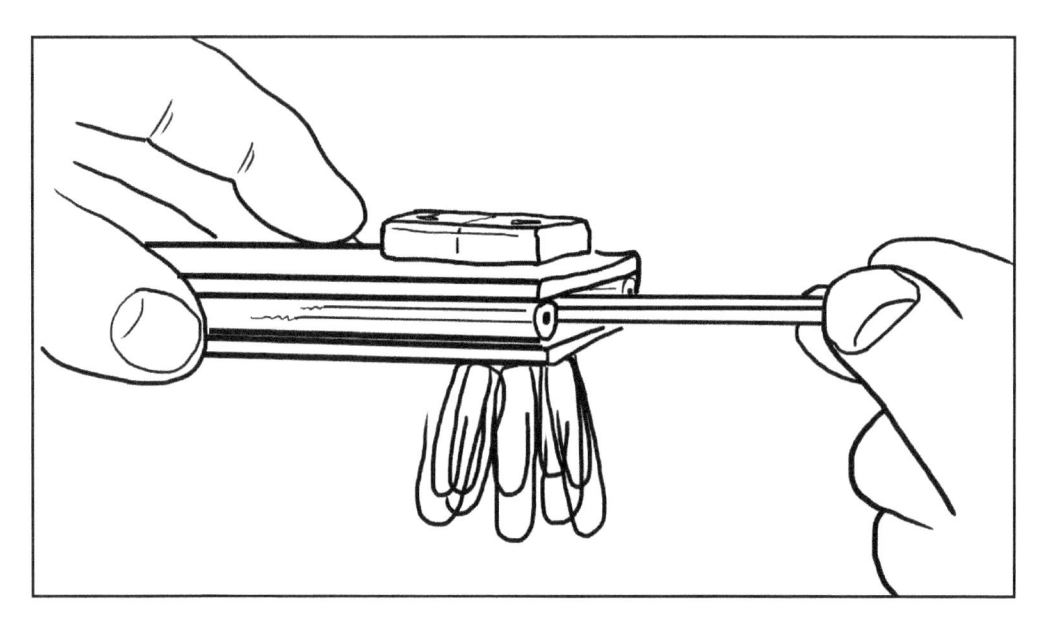

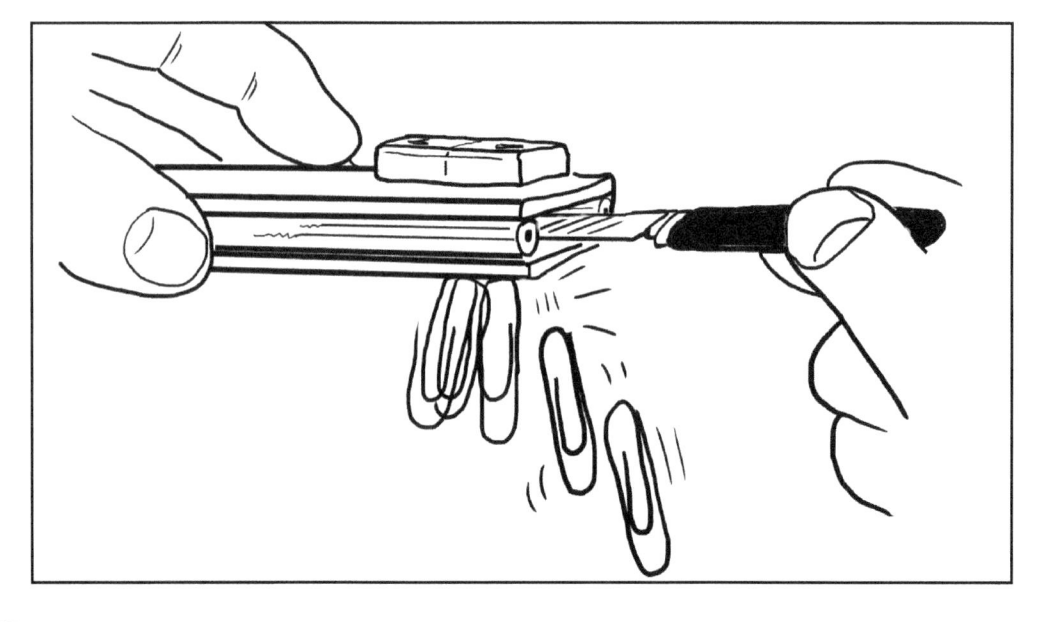

cardboard

paperclips

wooden stick

magnet

knife

PCM P3: **Recycling aluminium**

Make a chart about recycling aluminium.

Use the stages that you saw in the video.

You should include:

- collection of waste cans
- separation of steel cans from aluminium cans using magnets
- crushing
- melting
- rolling new metal sheet
- making new cans.

The process should be a loop, with the end of the recycling process also being the beginning.

Include the reduce, reuse, recycle symbol. Explain the ways in which recycling is good for our environment.

Topic 1 Humans and animals

Biology: Assessment Sheet B1

1 Tick (✓) two statements that describe the properties of bones.

   a Bones are very heavy. ☐

   b Bones are very light. ☐

   c Most bones are hollow. ☐

   d Most bones are weak. ☐   [2 marks]

2 Write three functions of the human skeleton.

   _____

   _____

   _____   [3 marks]

3 Look at this diagram of a leg.

   a What are parts labelled a to d called?

   b When the knee straightens, which muscle contracts and bunches up? Which muscle relaxes and stretches out?   [3 marks]

4 Describe how a muscle causes a bone to move.

   _____

   _____   [2 marks]

[Total: _____ /10]

Topic 1 Humans and animals

Biology: Assessment Sheet B2

1 Draw lines to join the names of the bones to the correct place on the picture.

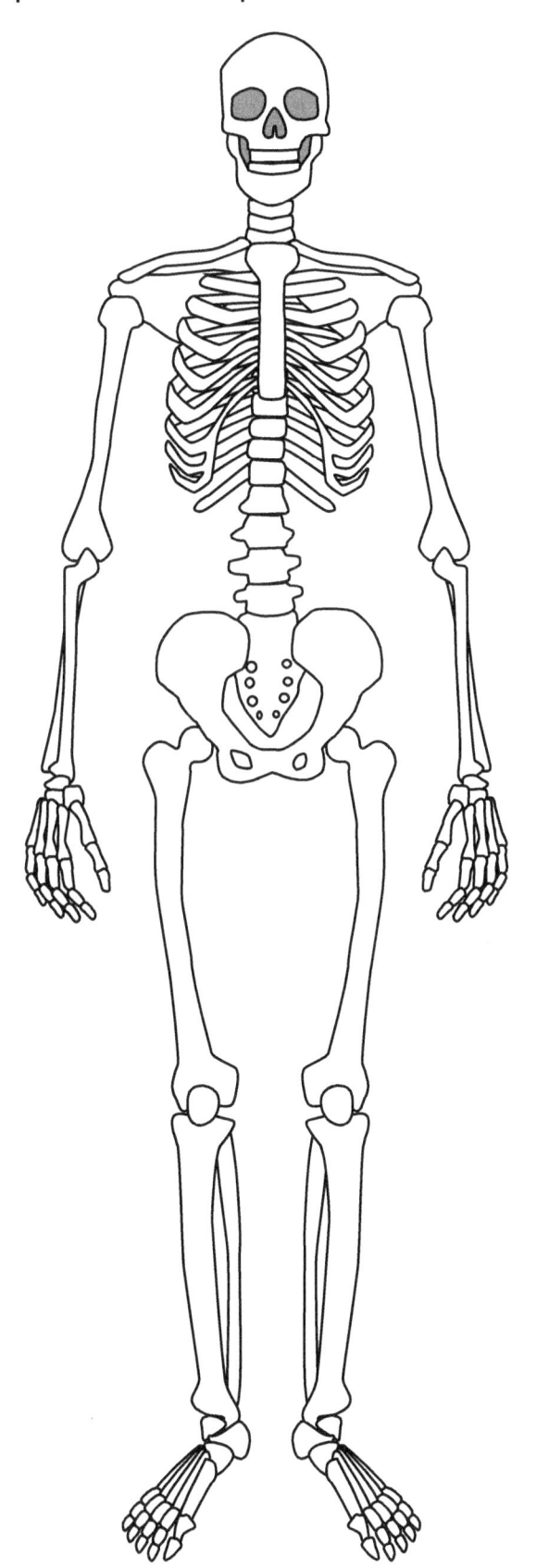

spine

skull

thigh bone

ribs

[4 marks]

continued

Stage 4 Collins Primary Science 2014

Topic 1 Humans and animals

Biology: Assessment Sheet B2 (continued)

2 Complete the sentences using the words in the box.

| supports | skeleton | move | rigid |

Bones are hard and strong and they form a _____ frame inside your body. This frame of bones is called your _____. Your skeleton helps you to _____ and _____ your body, as well as protecting the soft parts inside your body. [4 marks]

3 Write how many bones there are in an adult human skeleton.

_____   [1 mark]

4 Name one animal that does not have any bones.

_____   [1 mark]

[Total: _____ /10]

Topic 1 Humans and animals

Biology: Assessment Sheet B3

1 Circle the correct words.

Our muscles are attached to our bones by **ligaments / tendons**. The **weakest / strongest** muscles are the muscles you use to bite things. They are found on either side of your mouth. The most active muscles are the six muscles that move the **eye / ear** around in its socket. Your heart is a special kind of muscle that never gets **used / tired**. [4 marks]

2 Read the statements. Circle either 'True' or 'False'.

a A baby has more bones than an adult. TRUE / FALSE

b Bones are alive and they grow and change as we grow and change. TRUE / FALSE [2 marks]

3 Look at the pictures. Colour in the muscles so the ones that are relaxed are blue and the ones that have contracted are red.

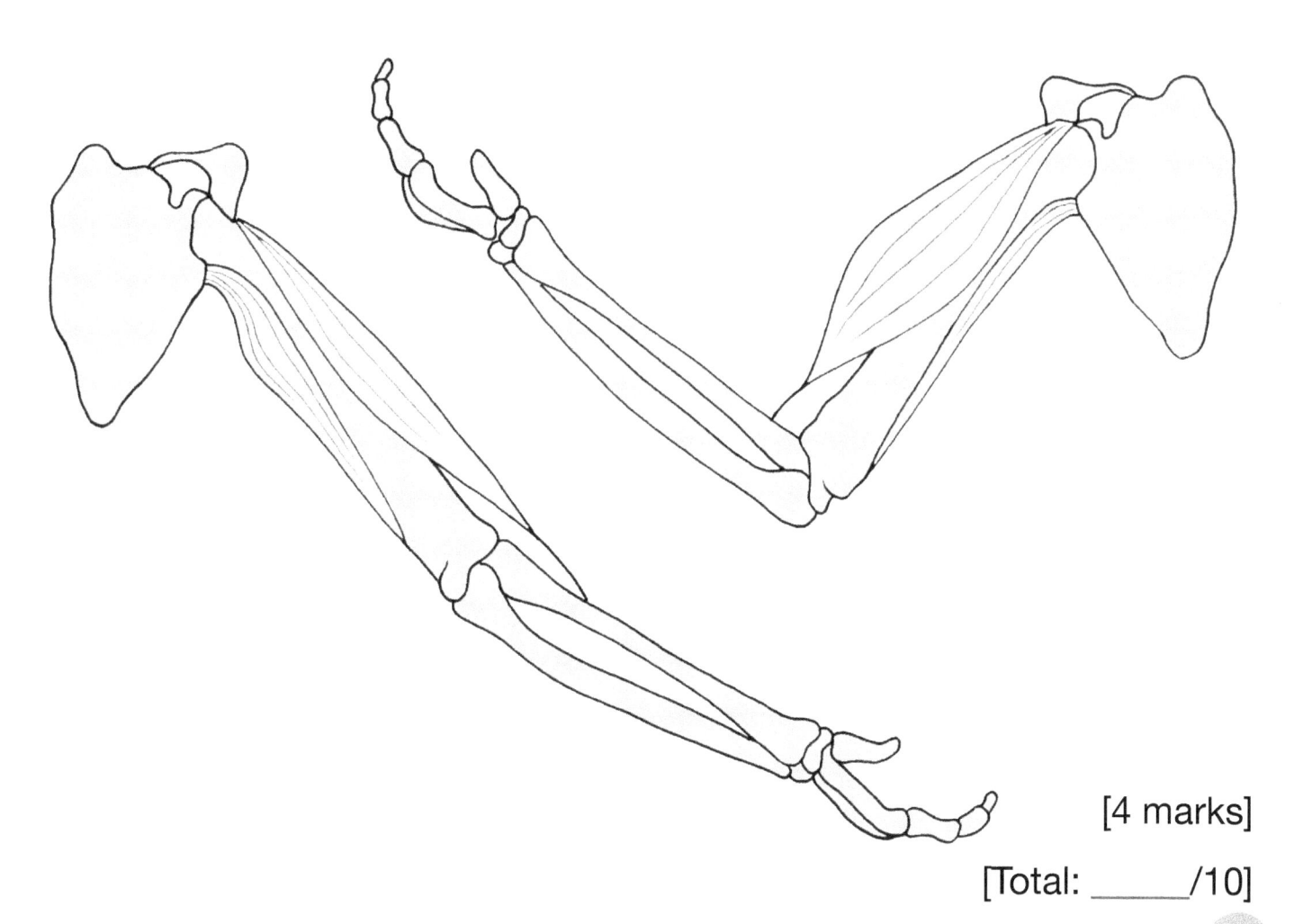

[4 marks]

[Total: _____/10]

Stage 4 Collins Primary Science 2014 105

Topic 1 Humans and animals

Biology: Assessment Sheet B4

1 Read the statements. Circle either 'True' or 'False'.

   a You can use an inhaler to treat and control asthma.
   TRUE / FALSE

   b Antibiotics can be used to treat bacterial infections.
   TRUE / FALSE

   c Aspirin is made from a plant.   TRUE / FALSE   [3 marks]

2 Draw lines to match up the beginning and end of each sentence.

   Drugs that are used to treat

   A drug is any substance

   Medicines can be

   dangerous if they are not used correctly.

   that affects how your body works.

   illness are called medicines.   [3 marks]

3 Complete the sentences using the words in the box.

   prescription   pharmacy

   A doctor gives a patient a _____ for the medicines

   to treat or prevent an illness. You have to take the prescription

   to a _____ or a clinic to get the medicines.   [2 marks]

4 Underline the correct words in these sentences.

   Some medicines are used to prevent us from becoming **old / ill**.

   Vaccines are often given to children and young babies so that

   they become **immune / attracted** to the disease.   [2 marks]

   [Total: _____/10]

Topic 1 Humans and animals

Biology: Assessment Sheet B5

1 Explain how each part of the giraffe helps it to survive.

Feature of giraffe	The way it helps the giraffe to survive
neck	
legs	
coat	

[3 marks]

2 Draw lines to match up the parts of a polar bear to the way each is adapted to suit its habitat.

claws   These are wide and flat to help the polar bear to walk on the snow.

paws   These are curved to help the polar bear to grip the ice.

fur   This provides camouflage.

nose   This is very sensitive to allow the polar bear to find other animals to hunt.

[4 marks]

3 Describe two ways a monkey is adapted to live in a forest.

_____

_____ [2 marks]

4 Name one animal that is suited to a pond habitat.

_____ [1 mark]

[Total: _____ /10]

Stage 4 Collins Primary Science 2014

Topic 2 Living things in their environment

Biology: Assessment Sheet B6

1 Write the names of the four animals in the correct place in the key.

   cricket   woodlouse   centipede   caterpillar

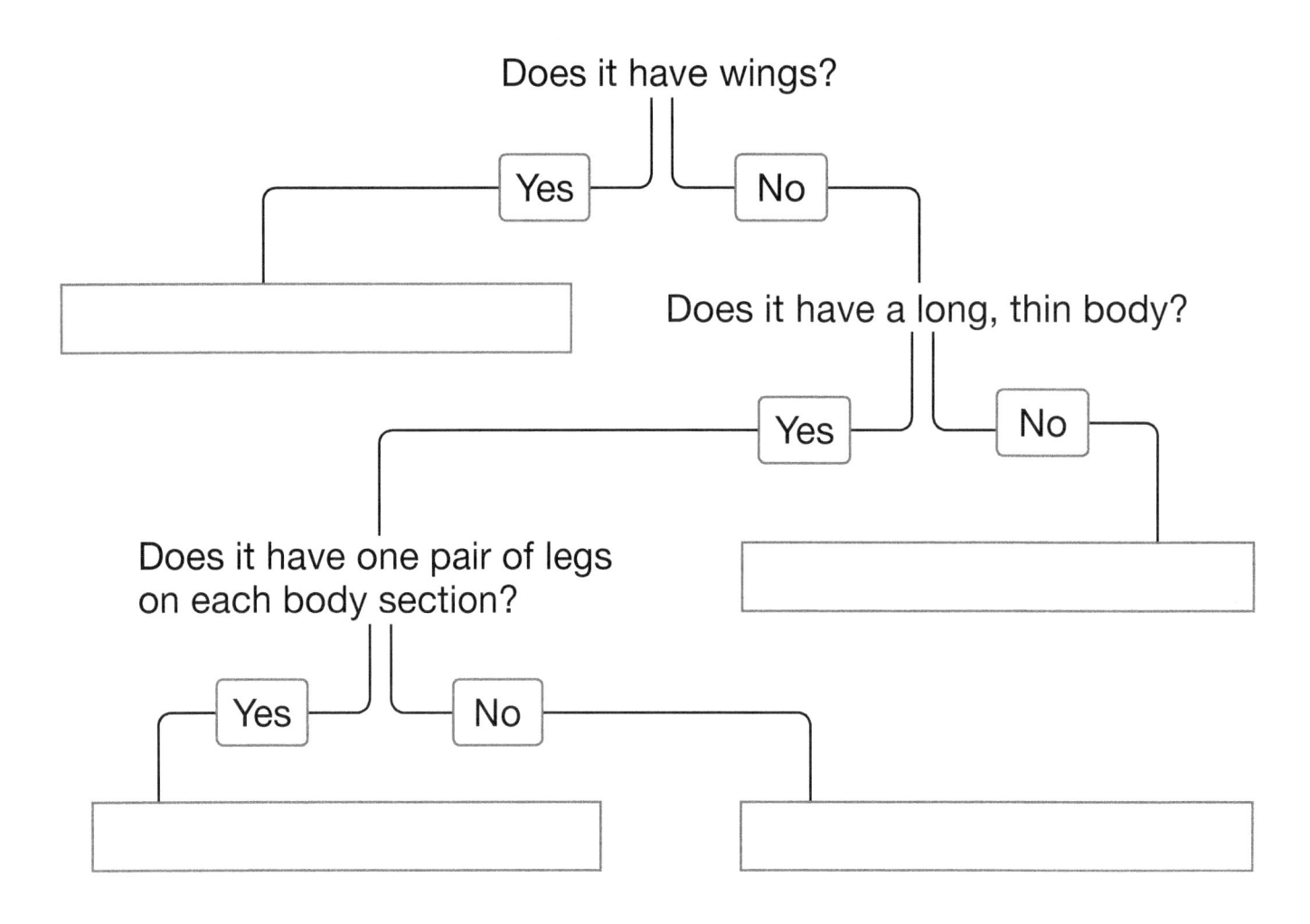

   Does it have wings?
   - Yes
   - No

   Does it have a long, thin body?
   - Yes
   - No

   Does it have one pair of legs on each body section?
   - Yes
   - No

   [4 marks]

2 Name one difference between:

   a spider and a caterpillar _____

   a slug and a woodlouse _____

   an owl and a duck _____   [3 marks]

   continued ➡

108   Stage 4 Collins Primary Science 2014

Biology: **Assessment Sheet B6 (continued)**

3 Read the statements. Circle either 'True' or 'False'.

   a You can use a simple key to identify different living things.

                              TRUE / FALSE

   b Living things cannot be classified into different groups.

                              TRUE / FALSE

   c The differences between animals in a group can be used to identify them.

                              TRUE / FALSE   [3 marks]

                                            [Total: _____/10]

Topic 2 Living things in their environment

Biology: Assessment Sheet B7

1 Describe two effects of water pollution.

   _____

   _____ [2 marks]

2 Read the statements. Circle either 'True' or 'False'.

   a Oil spilled in the ocean only affects the small fish.

      TRUE / FALSE

   b Oil spilled in the ocean can prevent seabirds from being able to fly.   TRUE / FALSE   [2 marks]

3 Circle the correct words.

   People can leave a lot of **rubbish / clothes** behind them after they visit natural environments. Plastic can take hundreds of years to disappear. It looks untidy and it can be very **helpful / harmful** to animals too. Everyone should take their **waste / water** home after a day out.   [3 marks]

4 Look at this list. Draw a circle around the things that can be recycled.

   newspaper   drinks can   polystyrene   glass   [3 marks]

   [Total: _____ /10]

Chemistry: Assessment Sheet C1

1 Draw lines to match the word with its description.

solid   takes the shape of any container, can flow and can be squashed

liquid   takes the shape of any container, can flow and cannot be squashed

gas   has a fixed shape, cannot flow and cannot be squashed   [3 marks]

2 Complete the table by writing either solid, liquid or gas.

Material	Solid, liquid or gas?
puddle	
glass bottle	
air	
ice cube	
oil	

[5 marks]

3 Describe two ways we can show that gases exist.

_____

_____ [2 marks]

[Total: ____/10]

Chemistry: Assessment Sheet C2

1 Circle the correct words.

Water is a very common type of matter and it exists in all **two / three** states. Running or flowing water is in a **solid / liquid** state. Ice is water in a **solid / gaseous** state. You cannot see water or smell water in its gaseous state because water gas is invisible and odourless. However, there is water **solid / gas** in the air around you all the time. We call water gas in the air water vapour.   [4 marks]

2 Read the statements. Circle either 'True' or 'False'.

a When matter changes from solid to liquid or from liquid to gas, we say it has undergone a change of state.
TRUE / FALSE

b Evaporation is the change of state from a liquid to a solid.   TRUE / FALSE

c Melting and freezing are reverse processes.
TRUE / FALSE   [3 marks]

3 Draw lines from the labels to the correct places on the diagram.

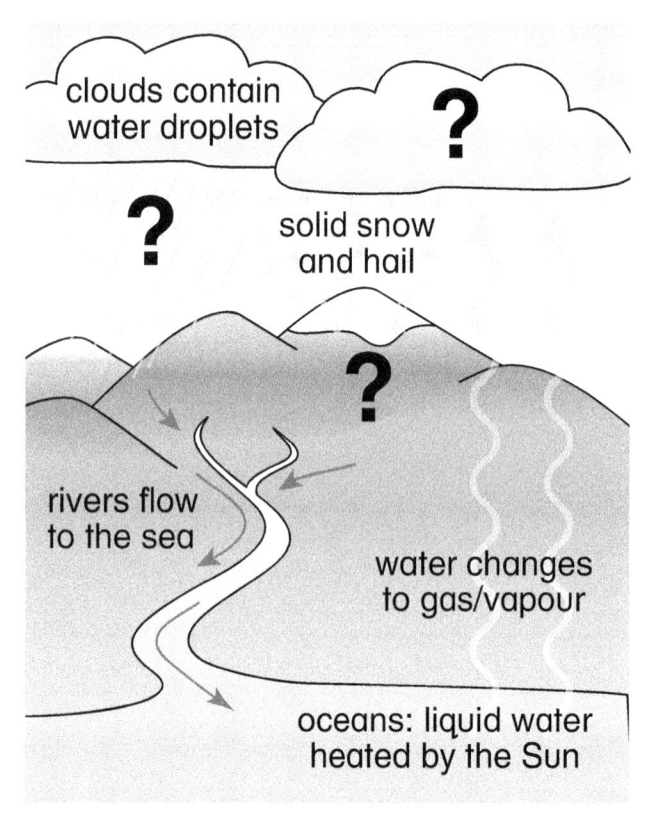

Gas cools and forms clouds.

Snow melts and liquid runs off.

Rain from clouds falls to earth.

[3 marks]

[Total: _____ /10]

Topic 3 States of matter

Chemistry: Assessment Sheet C3

1 Complete the table to show how different factors speed up or slow down evaporation.

Factor	Speed up or slow down evaporation?
Increased temperature	
Less airflow	
Increased surface area	

[3 marks]

2 Complete the sentences using the words in the box.

| solid   evaporates   liquid   freezing   melted |

When you warm up solids, such as ice or butter, they get soft and then turn to _____. When solids change state and become liquid we say they have _____. When a liquid is cooled enough, it turns to a _____. We say it solidifies, or freezes. _____ is the reverse of melting. When water in liquid state is heated it _____ and turns to a gas.   [5 marks]

3 Tick the sentences that are true. Cross the sentences that are false.

a Water vapour and steam will turn back into water when they are cooled. This process is called condensation.

b Water turns to steam when it is boiled. When the steam is cooled, it melts.

[2 marks]

[Total: ____/10]

Stage 4 Collins Primary Science 2014   113

Topic 4 Sound

Physics: Assessment Sheet P1

1 Read the statements. Circle either 'True' or 'False'.

   a Sound cannot travel through solids or liquids.
   TRUE / FALSE

   b The loudness of a sound is called the volume of the sound.
   TRUE / FALSE

   c Sound is measured in units called newtons.
   TRUE / FALSE   [3 marks]

2 Here are some of the speeds at which sound travels:
   330 m/s through air   1430 m/s in water   3600 m/s through steel.

   a Through which state of matter does sound travel the slowest? _____

   b Through which state of matter does sound travel the fastest? _____   [2 marks]

3 Describe what is vibrating to cause the sounds in each of the musical instruments below.

   _____   _____   _____   _____

   _____   _____   _____   _____

   [4 marks]

4 Complete this sentence. Use the words in the box to help you.

   | metres per second   kilometres per hour   decibels per minute |

   We measure the speed at which sound travels in

   _____ (m/s).   [1 mark]

   [Total: _____/10]

114   Stage 4 Collins Primary Science 2014

Topic 4 Sound

Physics: Assessment Sheet P2

1 Read the statements. Circle either 'True' or 'False'.

   a Pitch describes how high or low a
   sound is.   TRUE / FALSE

   b Wave patterns can tell us about the pitch
   and loudness of a sound.   TRUE / FALSE

   c Sounds of the same pitch can only
   be loud.   TRUE / FALSE

   d Some materials absorb vibrations, which allows
   more sound to travel through them.   TRUE / FALSE   [4 marks]

2 This factory worker wears ear protectors.

   a Why is it important to stop loud sounds with ear protectors?

   _____

   b Explain how ear protectors reduce the volume of a sound.

   _____

   _____ [2 marks]

3 Circle the correct words.
   Sounds can differ in **weight / volume**. We measure loudness
   in decibels. Sounds can also be high or low, depending
   on the speed of the **vibration / music**. The highness or
   lowness of sounds is called the **pitch / play** of the sound.
   For example, an emergency siren is a high-pitched sound
   and the roll of thunder is a **low / light** pitched sound.   [4 marks]

   [Total: _____/10]

   Stage 4 Collins Primary Science 2014   115

Topic 5 Electricity and magnetism

Physics: Assessment Sheet P3

1 Draw lines to match the names of the components to the pictures.

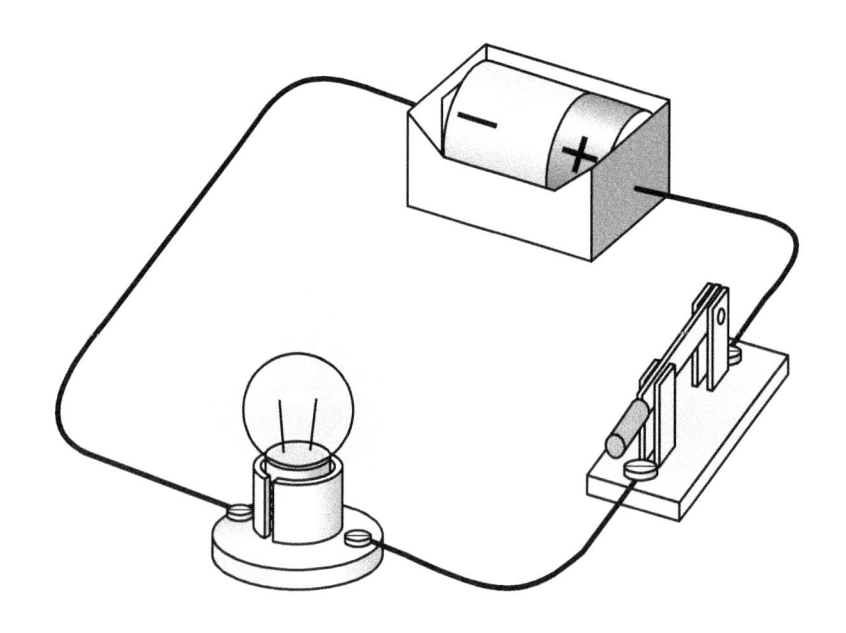

lamp   lamp holder   switch   cell   wire

[5 marks]

2 Read the statements. Circle either 'True' or 'False'.

   a Circuits are built by connecting components
      to form a broken circuit.   TRUE / FALSE

   b If there is a break in the circuit, the device
      will still work.   TRUE / FALSE   [2 marks]

3 Circle the correct words.

   In a circuit the battery gives electrical energy. To make

   the lamps brighter we can use **more / smaller** batteries.

   This makes the lights brighter because there is more

   energy / wires. However, if the circuit is

   complete / broken the lamp will not light up.   [3 marks]

[Total: _____/10]

Topic 5 Electricity and magnetism

Physics: Assessment Sheet P4

1 Draw lines to match up the beginning and end of each sentence.

A switch is used	allows electricity to flow around it.
Electrical current	to stop the electricity flowing in a circuit.
A circuit is a closed path which	flows around a circuit in a continuous loop.

[3 marks]

2 Complete the sentences using the words in the box.

electrons   wires   particles   flow

Electricity has to travel from the battery along the _____ and through the lamp in order to make it work. The _____ of electricity through the circuit is called an electric current. We cannot see the current, so we have to use models to describe how it flows. You can think of an electric current as a flow of tiny _____ (called _____) though the wire. [4 marks]

3 In which circuit, A or B, will the lamps not light up? ____

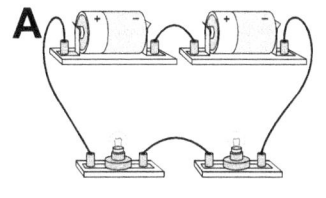

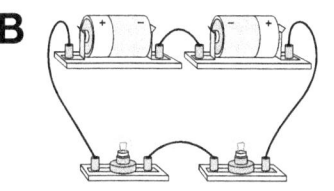

A   B

[1 mark]

4 Read the statements. Circle either 'True' or 'False'.

   a Electrical components do not need a complete circuit to work.   TRUE / FALSE

   b In a complete circuit the lamp(s) will light up.
                                    TRUE / FALSE   [2 marks]

[Total: _____/10]

Stage 4 Collins Primary Science 2014   117

Topic 5 Electricity and magnetism

Physics: Assessment Sheet P5

1 Draw a line from each of the labels below to the correct place on the diagram.

   the part that would repel another magnet's N pole

   the place where the magnetic field is strongest

   the S pole

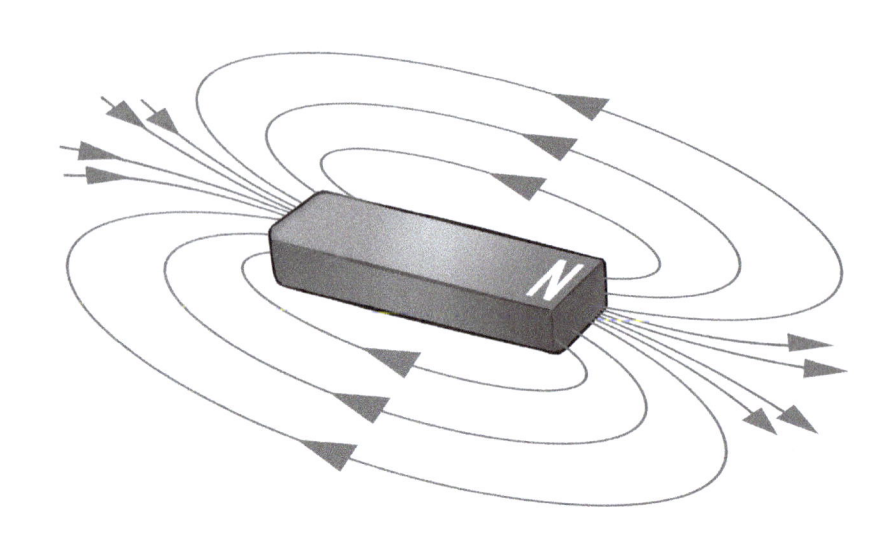

   [3 marks]

2 Circle the correct words.

   Magnets can be used to **separate / join** magnetic materials from non-magnetic materials. This is particularly useful in industries where metals are thrown **away / recycled**. [2 marks]

3 Tick the metals that are magnetic.

   steel ☐   gold ☐   iron ☐   aluminium ☐   [2 marks]

4 Read the statements. Circle either 'True' or 'False'.

   a The force exerted by a magnet is strongest at its poles.
   TRUE / FALSE

   b When like poles are facing each other, the magnets attract each other.
   TRUE / FALSE

   c Magnets attract all metals.   TRUE / FALSE   [3 marks]

   [Total: ____/10]

118 Stage 4 Collins Primary Science 2014